AFRO-AMERICAN LITERATURE

○ Fiction
○ Drama
○ Poetry
● Nonfiction

AFRO-AMERICAN LITERATURE:

HOUGHTON MIFFLIN COMPANY • BOSTON
New York • Atlanta • Geneva, Illinois • Dallas • Palo Alto

NONFICTION

William Adams
Peter Conn
Barry Slepian

Photo Credits

Printed in the U.S.A.

Contents

Acknowledgments

Grateful acknowledgment is made to authors, publishers, and agents for their permission to reprint the following selections.

"Black Pawns in a White Game," reprinted from *Look Out, Whitey! Black Power's Gon' Get Your Mama* by Julius Lester. Copyright © 1968 by Julius Lester and used by permission of the publisher, The Dial Press, Inc.

"Cast Down Your Bucket Where You Are" by Booker T. Washington. From *In Their Own Words: A History of the American Negro 1865–1916*, by Milton Meltzer. Copyright © 1965 by Milton Meltzer. Thomas Y. Crowell Company, New York, publishers.

FROM *The Autobiography of W. E. B. DuBois* by W. E. B. DuBois. Copyright 1968 by International Publishers Co., Inc. Reprinted by permission of International Publishers Co., Inc.

FROM *Letters to a Black Boy* by Bob Teague, published by Walker & Company, New York. Copyright © 1968 by Robert L. Teague.

FROM *The Life of Frederick Douglass*, published by The New American Library, Inc.

FROM *Manchild in the Promised Land* by Claude Brown. Reprinted with permission of The Macmillan Company. Copyright © Claude Brown, 1965.

FROM "Mascot," a selection from *The Autobiography of Malcolm X*, by Malcolm X with the assistance of Alex Haley. Reprinted by permission of Grove Press, Inc. Copyright © 1964 by Alex Haley and Malcolm X. Copyright © 1965 by Alex Haley and Betty Shabazz.

FROM "The Movement," reprinted from *Coming of Age in Mississippi* by Anne Moody. Copyright © 1968 by Anne Moody and used by permission of the publisher, The Dial Press, Inc.

"I Have a Dream" by Martin Luther King, Jr. Copyright © 1963 by Martin Luther King, Jr. Reprinted by permission of Joan Daves.

"The Man Who Went to Chicago," reprinted from *Eight Men* by Richard Wright. Copyright © 1945 by L. B. Fischer Publishing Corporation under the title *Early Days in Chicago*. Reprinted by permission of Paul R. Reynolds, Inc.

"Negroes Have a Right to Fight Back," by John Oliver Killens, from *Saturday Evening Post*, July 2, 1966. Reprinted by permission of International Famous Agency, Inc. and the *Saturday Evening Post*. Copyright © 1966 Curtis Publishing Company.

"Notes of a Native Son," reprinted from *Notes of a Native Son* by James Baldwin. Copyright © 1955 by James Baldwin. Used by permission of The Beacon Press.

"Not Poor, Just Broke," from the book *nigger: An Autobiography* by Dick Gregory with Robert Lipsyte. Copyright © 1964 by Dick Gregory Enterprises, Inc. Reprinted by permission of E. P. Dutton & Co., Inc.

"A Southern Tale," from *Freedom — When?*, by James Farmer. Copyright © 1965 by the Congress of Racial Equality, Inc. Reprinted by permission of Random House, Inc.

"Tokenism: 300 Years for Five Cents," from *Home: Social Essays* by LeRoi Jones. Reprinted by permission of William Morrow and Company, Inc. Copyright © 1962, 1966 by LeRoi Jones.

"The White Race and Its Heroes," from *Soul on Ice* by Eldridge Cleaver. Copyright © 1968 by Eldridge Cleaver. Used with permission of McGraw-Hill Book Company.

For Our Sons

Rusty Adams
Steven and David Conn
John Slepian

Early
Spokesmen

Frederick Douglass

(*1817–1895*)

Born a slave in Talbot County, Maryland, Frederick Douglass became a house servant at the age of eight and learned reading and writing from his master's wife. In 1838, Douglass escaped slavery and fled to New York disguised as a sailor. He was later accused of conspiring with John Brown in the revolt at Harper's Ferry and sought refuge for a time in Canada. Douglass was an active leader in the antislavery movement in America, and after the Civil War he was an ardent worker for civil rights. Author of several "slave narratives," Douglass wrote three autobiographies, of which *Narrative of the Life of Frederick Douglass, an American Slave* is best known. Douglass lectured in Britain, served as president of Freedman's Savings Bank and held many official positions in government during Reconstruction. He was the U.S. Marshal of the District of Columbia under President Hayes and eventually became Minister to Haiti. He also served at one time as chargé d'affaires to Santo Domingo, and he was Lincoln's advisor in determining the role of the black man in the Civil War. Douglass viewed freedom as the "foundation of all manly virtue," and he was a significant contributor to the black man's fight for freedom. He felt that the Bill of Rights was for black people a "bill of wrongs," and he devoted his lifetime efforts to achieving equal rights for his race.

FROM

The Life of Frederick Douglass

I lived in Master Hugh's family about seven years. During this time, I succeeded in learning to read and write. In accomplishing this, I was compelled to resort to various stratagems. I had no regular teacher. My mistress, who had kindly commenced to instruct me, had, in compliance with the advice and direction of her husband, not only ceased to instruct, but had set her face against my being instructed by anyone else. It is due, however, to my mistress to say of her, that she did not adopt this course of treatment immediately. She at first lacked the depravity indispensable to shutting me up in mental darkness. It was at least necessary for her to have some training in the exercise of irresponsible power, to make her equal to the task of treating me as though I were a brute.

My mistress was, as I have said, a kind and tenderhearted woman; and in the simplicity of her soul she commenced, when I first went to live with her, to treat me as she supposed one human being ought to treat another. In entering upon the duties of a slaveholder, she did not seem to perceive that I sustained to her the relation of a mere chattel, and that for her to treat me as a human being was not only wrong, but dangerously so. Slavery proved as injurious to her as it did to me. When I went there, she was a pious, warm, and tenderhearted woman. There was no sorrow or suffering for which she had not a tear. She had bread for the hungry, clothes for the naked, and comfort for every mourner that came within her reach. Slavery soon proved its ability to divest her of these heavenly qualities. Under its influence, the

3

tender heart became stone, and the lamblike disposition gave way to one of tigerlike fierceness. The first step in her downward course was in her ceasing to instruct me. She now commenced to practice her husband's precepts. She finally became even more violent in her opposition than her husband himself. She was not satisfied with simply doing as well as he had commanded; she seemed anxious to do better. Nothing seemed to make her more angry than to see me with a newspaper. She seemed to think that here lay the danger. I have had her rush at me with a face made all up of fury, and snatch from me a newspaper, in a manner that fully revealed her apprehension. She was an apt woman; and a little experience soon demonstrated, to her satisfaction, that education and slavery were incompatible with each other.

From this time I was most narrowly watched. If I was in a separate room any considerable length of time, I was sure to be suspected of having a book, and was at once called to give an account of myself. All this, however, was too late. The first step had been taken. Mistress, in teaching me the alphabet, had given me the *inch*, and no precaution could prevent me from taking the *ell*.

The plan which I adopted, and the one by which I was most successful, was that of making friends of all the little white boys whom I met in the street. As many of these as I could, I converted into teachers. With their kindly aid, obtained at different times and in different places, I finally succeeded in learning to read. When I was sent on errands, I always took my book with me, and by doing one part of my errand quickly, I found time to get a lesson before my return. I used also to carry bread with me, enough of which was always in the house, and to which I was always welcome; for I was much better off in this regard than many of the poor white children in our neighborhood. This bread I used to bestow upon the hungry little urchins, who, in return, would give me that more valuable bread of knowledge. I am strongly tempted to give the names of two or three of those little boys, as a testimonial of the gratitude and affection I bear them; but prudence forbids; — not that it would injure me, but it might embarrass them; for it is almost an unpardonable offense to teach slaves to read in this Christian country. It is enough to say of the dear little fellows, that they lived on Philpot Street, very near

Durgin and Bailey's shipyard. I used to talk this matter of slavery over with them. I would sometimes say to them, I wished I could be as free as they would be when they got to be men. "You will be free as soon as you are twenty-one, *but I am a slave for life!* Have not I as good a right to be free as you have?" These words used to trouble them; they would express for me the liveliest sympathy, and console me with the hope that something would occur by which I might be free.

I was now about twelve years old, and the thought of being *a slave for life* began to bear heavily upon my heart. Just about this time, I got hold of a book entitled *The Columbian Orator.* Every opportunity I got, I used to read this book. Among much of other interesting matter, I found in it a dialogue between a master and his slave. The slave was represented as having run away from his master three times. The dialogue represented the conversation which took place between them, when the slave was retaken the third time. In this dialogue, the whole argument in behalf of slavery was brought forward by the master, all of which was disposed of by the slave. The slave was made to say some very smart as well as impressive things in reply to his master — things which had the desired though unexpected effect; for the conversation resulted in the voluntary emancipation of the slave on the part of the master.

In the same book, I met with one of Sheridan's mighty speeches on and in behalf of Catholic emancipation. These were choice documents to me. I read them over and over again with unabated interest. They gave tongue to interesting thoughts of my own soul, which had frequently flashed through my mind, and died away for want of utterance. The moral which I gained from the dialogue was the power of truth over the conscience of even a slaveholder. What I got from Sheridan was a bold denunciation of slavery, and a powerful vindication of human rights. The reading of these documents enabled me to utter my thoughts, and to meet the arguments brought forward to sustain slavery; but while they relieved me of one difficulty, they brought on another even more painful than the one of which I was relieved. The more I read, the more I was led to abhor and detest my enslavers. I could regard them in no other light than a band of successful robbers, who had left their homes, and gone to Africa, and stolen us from our homes, and in a strange land reduced us to slavery. I loathed them as being the meanest as well as the most wicked of men. As I read and contemplated the subject, behold! that very discontentment which Master Hugh had predicted would follow my learning to read had already come, to torment and sting my soul to unutterable anguish. As I writhed under it, I would at times feel that learning to read had been a curse rather than a blessing. It had given me a view of my wretched condition, without the remedy. It opened my eyes to the horrible pit, but to no ladder upon which to get out. In moments of agony, I envied my fellow slaves for their stupidity. I have often wished myself a beast. I preferred the condition of the meanest reptile to my own. Anything, no matter what, to get rid of thinking! It was this everlasting thinking of my condition that tormented me. There was no getting rid of it. It was pressed upon me by every object within sight or hearing, animate or inanimate. The silver trump of freedom had roused my soul to eternal wakefulness. Freedom now appeared, to disappear no more forever. It was heard in every sound, and seen in every thing. It was ever present to torment me with a sense of my wretched condition. I saw nothing without seeing it, I heard nothing without hearing it, and felt nothing without feeling it. It looked from every star, it smiled in every calm, breathed in every wind, and moved in every storm.

I often found myself regretting my own existence, and wishing myself dead; and but for the hope of being free, I have no doubt but that I should have killed myself, or done something for which I should have been killed. While in this state of mind, I was eager to hear anyone speak of slavery. I was a ready listener. Every little while, I could hear something about the abolitionists. It was some time before I found what the word meant. It was always used in such connections as to make it an interesting word to me. If a slave ran away and succeeded in getting clear, or if a slave killed his master, set fire to a barn, or did any thing very wrong in the mind of a slaveholder, it was spoken of as the fruit of *abolition.* Hearing the word in this connection very often, I set about learning what it meant. The dictionary afforded me little or no help. I found it was "the act of abolishing," but then I did not know what was to be abolished. Here I was perplexed. I did not dare to ask anyone about its meaning, for I was satisfied that it was something they wanted me to know very little about. After a patient waiting, I got one of our city papers, containing an account of the number of petitions from the North, praying for the abolition of slavery in the District of Columbia, and of the slave trade between the states. From this time I understood the words *abolition* and *abolitionist,* and always drew near when that word was spoken, expecting to hear something of importance to myself and fellow slaves. The light broke in upon me by degrees. I went one day down on the wharf of Mr. Waters, and seeing two Irishmen unloading a scow of stone, I went, unasked, and helped them. When we had finished, one of them came to me and asked me if I were a slave. I told him I was. He asked, "Are ye a slave for life?" I told him that I was. The good Irishman seemed to be deeply affected by the statement. He said to the other that it was a pity so fine a little fellow as myself should be a slave for life. He said it was a shame to hold me. They both advised me to run away to the North; that I should find friends there, and that I should be free. I pretended not to be interested in what they said and treated them as if I did not understand them, for I feared they might be treacherous. White men have been known to encourage slaves to escape, and then, to get the reward, catch them and return them to their masters. I was afraid that these seemingly good men might use me so; but nevertheless remembered their advice, and from that time I resolved to run away. I looked forward to a time at which it would be safe for me to escape. I was too young to think of doing so immediately; besides, I wished to learn how to write, as I might have occasion to write my own pass. I consoled myself with the hope that I should one day find a good chance. Meanwhile, I would learn to write.

The idea as to how I might learn to write was suggested to me by being in Durgin and Bailey's shipyard, and frequently seeing the ship carpenters, after hewing, and getting a piece of timber ready for use, write on the timber the name of that part of the ship for which it was intended. When a piece of timber was intended for the larboard side, it would be marked thus — "L." When a piece was for the starboard side, it would be marked thus — "S." A piece for the larboard side forward would be marked thus — "L. F." When a piece was for starboard side forward, it would be marked thus — "S. F." For larboard aft, it would be marked thus — "L. A." For starboard aft, it would be marked thus — "S. A." I soon learned the names of these letters, and for what they were intended when placed upon a piece of timber in the shipyard. I immediately commenced copying them, and in a short time was able to make the four letters named. After that, when I met with any boy who I knew could write, I would tell him I could write as well as he. The next word would be, "I don't believe you. Let me see you try it." I would then make the letters which I had been so fortunate as to learn, and ask him to beat that. In this way I got a good many lessons in writing, which it is quite possible I should never have gotten in any other way. During this time, my copybook was the board fence, brick wall, and pavement; my pen and ink was a lump of chalk. With these, I learned mainly how to write. I then commenced and continued copying the italics in *Webster's Spelling Book,* until I could make them all without looking on the book. By this time, my little Master Thomas had gone to school, and learned how to write, and had written over a number of copybooks. These had been brought home, and shown to some of our near neighbors, and then laid aside. My mistress used to go to class meeting at the Wilk Street meetinghouse every Monday afternoon, and leave me to take care of the house. When left thus, I used to spend the time in writing in the spaces left in Master Thomas's copybook, copying what he had written. I continued to do this until I could write a hand very similar to that of Master Thomas. Thus, after a long, tedious effort for years, I finally succeeded in learning how to write.

FOR DISCUSSION

1. In this selection, Douglass describes how owning a slave has a degrading effect on his mistress' character. Do you think that owning a slave would generally have such an effect? Why?
2. Douglass says it was "not only wrong, but dangerously so" to treat a slave like a human being. What does he mean?

Booker T. Washington
(1856–1915)

During the years following the Reconstruction period in the South, Booker T. Washington became a proponent of the belief that black people should help themselves through education rather than political demands. During his childhood he worked in a salt-furnace to help support his family, and he attended school at night. He learned about Hampton Institute in Virginia, a school for blacks, and at seventeen he set out to obtain an education; working as a janitor to pay for his board, he managed to learn the trade of brick masonry. After graduation he taught in segregated schools in Virginia and Washington, D.C., before he returned to Hampton as secretary to the principal. When plans were established for a teacher-training school at Tuskegee, Washington became founder and director. The school grew during Washington's lifetime from its original enrollment of forty students to a well-endowed institution teaching thirty-eight trades and professions to over fifteen hundred students. As a result of his efforts on behalf of educational advancement for black people in America, Washington was honored by many world leaders, including President Theodore Roosevelt. Author of many published works, including *Up from Slavery, My Larger Education, The Future of the American Negro, Putting the Most into Life,* and *The Man Farthest Down,* Washington insisted that "No man, black or white, from North or South, shall drag me down so low as to make me hate him."

Cast Down Your Bucket Where You Are

(Speech at The Cotton States Exposition, Atlanta, 1895)

A ship lost at sea for many days suddenly sighted a friendly vessel. From the mast of the unfortunate vessel was seen the signal: "Water, water, we die of thirst." The answer from the friendly vessel at once came back, "Cast down your bucket where you are." A second time the signal, "Water, water, send us water," ran up from the distressed vessel and was answered, "Cast down your bucket where you are," and a third and fourth signal for water was answered "Cast down your bucket where you are." The captain of the distressed vessel, at last heeding the injunction, cast down his bucket and it came up full of fresh, sparkling water from the mouth of the Amazon River. To those of my race who depend on bettering their condition in a foreign land, or who underestimate the importance of cultivating friendly relations with the Southern white man who is their next door neighbor, I would say, cast down your bucket where you are, cast it down in making friends, in every manly way, of the people of all races by whom you are surrounded. Cast it down in agriculture, in mechanics, in commerce, in domestic service, and in the professions. And in this connection it is well to bear in mind that, whatever other sins the South may be called upon to bear, when it comes to business pure and simple it is in the South that the Negro is given a man's chance in the commercial world; and in nothing is this Exposition more eloquent than in emphasizing this chance. Our greatest danger is, that, in the great leap from slavery to freedom, we may overlook the fact that the masses of us are to live by the productions of our hands, and fail to keep in mind that we shall prosper in the proportion as we learn to dignify and glorify common labor and put brains and skill into the common occupations of life; shall prosper in proportion as we learn to draw the line between the superficial and the substantial, the ornamental gewgaws of life and the useful. No race can prosper till it learns that there is as much dignity in tilling a field as in writing a poem. It is at the bottom of life we must begin and not the top. Nor should we permit our grievances to overshadow our opportunities.

To those of the white race who look to the incoming of those of foreign birth and strange tongue and habits for the prosperity of the South, were I permitted, I would repeat what I say to my own race, "Cast down your bucket where you are." Cast it down among the 8,000,000 Negroes whose habits you know, whose loyalty and love you have tested in days when to have proved treacherous meant the ruin of your firesides. Cast it down among those people who have, without strikes and labor wars, tilled your fields, cleared your forests, builded your railroads and cities, and brought forth treasures from the bowels of the earth and helped make possible this magnificent representation of the progress of the South. Casting down your bucket among my people, helping and encouraging as you are doing on these grounds, and with education of head, hand and heart, you will find that they will buy your surplus land, make blossom the waste places in your fields, and run your factories. While doing this you can be sure in the future, as you have been in the past, that you and your families will be surrounded by the most patient, faithful, law-abiding, and unresentful people that the world has seen. As we have proved our loyalty to you in the past, in nursing your children, watching by the sick beds of your mothers and fathers, and often following them with tear-dimmed eyes to their graves, so in the future, in our humble way, we shall stand by you with a devotion that no foreigner can approach, ready to lay down our lives, if need be, in defense of yours; interlacing our industrial, commercial, civil, and religious life with yours in a way that shall make the interests of both races one. In all things that are purely social we can be as separate as the fingers, yet one as the hand in all things essential to mutual progress.

There is no defense or security for any of us except in the highest intelligence and development of all. If anywhere there are efforts tending to curtail the fullest growth of the Negro, let these efforts be turned into stimulating, encouraging, and making him the most useful and intelligent citizen. Effort or means so invested will pay a thousand per cent interest. These efforts will be twice blessed — "blessing him that gives and him that takes."

There is no escape, through law of man or God, from the inevitable:

> *The laws of changeless justice bind*
> *Oppressor with oppressed,*
> *And close as sin and suffering joined*
> *We march to fate abreast.*

Nearly sixteen millions of hands will aid you pulling the load upwards, or they will pull against you the load downwards. We shall constitute one-third and much more of the ignorance and crime of the South, or one-third its intelligence and progress; we shall contribute one-third to the business and industrial prosperity of the South, or we shall prove a veritable body of death, stagnating, depressing, retarding every effort to advance the body politic.

The wisest among my race understand that the agitation of questions of social equality is the extremest folly, and the progress in the enjoyment of all the privileges that will come to us must be the result of severe and constant struggle, rather than of artificial forcing. No race that has anything to contribute to the markets of the world is long in any degree ostracized. It is important that we be prepared for the exercise of these privileges. The opportunity to earn a dollar in a factory just now is worth infinitely more than the opportunity to spend a dollar in an opera house.

In conclusion, may I repeat, that nothing in thirty years has given us more hope and encouragement and drawn us so near to you of the white race as the opportunity offered by this Exposition; here bending, as it were, over the altar that represents the results of the struggles of your race and mine, both starting practically empty-handed three decades ago, I pledge that, in your effort to work out the great and intricate problem which God has laid at the doors of the South, you shall have at all times the patient, sympathetic help of my race. Only let this be constantly in mind, that while, from representations in these buildings of the products of field, of forest, of mine, of factory, letters and art, much good will come — yet, far above and beyond material benefit, will be that higher good, that let us pray God will come, in a blotting out of sectional differences and racial animosities and suspicions, and in a determination, even in the remotest corner, to administer absolute justice; in a willing obedience among all classes to the mandates of law, and a spirit that will tolerate nothing but the highest equity in the enforcement of law. This, this, coupled with material prosperity, will bring into our beloved South new heaven and new earth.

FOR DISCUSSION

1. Washington expresses the hope that the philosophy he outlines in this speech will lead to "absolute justice." Do you think it could? This speech was delivered three decades after Emancipation. What evidence of progress does Washington offer?
2. Washington exhorts black people to concentrate their efforts on common labor, to "begin at the bottom." Do you think this is good advice?
3. Washington seems to accept the idea of racial separation. What do you think are his motives? How are they different from those of some contemporary black leaders who advocate separatism?

W. E. B. DuBois
(1868–1963)

An ardent civil rights worker, author, editor, and scholar, W. E. B. DuBois believed that "the problem of the Twentieth Century is the problem of the color line." During his long lifetime, he championed human rights and was a spokesman for Africa and for the world. DuBois was educated at Fisk, Harvard, and the University of Berlin; he taught history and economics in several universities, including Atlanta University. When he retired from teaching, DuBois helped to set up and direct the NAACP. An individualist with varied interests, DuBois once ran for New York Senator on the American Labor Party ticket. Best known for his writing, DuBois founded, edited, and published *The Crisis,* the NAACP magazine. He wrote numerous pamphlets and books on Africa and edited the *Encyclopedia Africana* while living in Africa. He also wrote articles, historical and sociological books, poems, autobiography, and novels in a style of poetic prose which has inspired both writers and artists. Among the best known of his works are *The Souls of Black Folk, Black Reconstruction,* and *Dusk at Dawn.* DuBois died in Ghana at the age of ninety-five.

FROM

The Autobiography of W. E. B. DuBois

The men of the Niagara Movement, coming from the toil of the year's hard work, and pausing a moment from the earning of their daily bread, turn toward the nation and again ask in the name of ten million the privilege of a hearing. In the past year the work of the Negro hater has flourished in the land. Step by step the defenders of the rights of American citizens have retreated. The work of stealing the black man's ballot has progressed, and fifty and more representatives of stolen votes still sit in the nation's capital. Discrimination in travel and public accommodation has so spread that some of our weaker brethren are actually afraid to thunder against color discrimination as such and are simply whispering for ordinary decencies.

Against this the Niagara Movement eternally protests. We will not be satisfied to take one jot or tittle less than our full manhood rights. We claim for ourselves every single right that belongs to a freeborn American, political, civil, and social; and until we get these rights we will never cease to protest and assail the ears of America. The battle we wage is not for ourselves alone, but for all true Americans. It is a fight for ideals, lest this, our common fatherland, false to its founding, become in truth the land of the Thief and the home of the Slave — a byword and a hissing among the nations for its sounding pretensions and pitiful accomplishment.

17

Never before in the modern age has a great and civilized folk threatened to adopt so cowardly a creed in the treatment of its fellow citizens, born and bred on its soil. Stripped of verbiage and subterfuge and in its naked nastiness, the new American creed says: fear to let black men even try to rise lest they become the equals of the white. And this in the land that professes to follow Jesus Christ. The blasphemy of such a course is only matched by its cowardice.

In detail our demands are clear and unequivocal. First, we would vote; with the right to vote goes everything: freedom, manhood, the honor of our wives, the chastity of our daughters, the right to work, and the chance to rise, and let no man listen to those who deny this.

We want full manhood suffrage, and we want it now, henceforth and forever.

Second. We want discrimination in public accommodation to cease. Separation in railway and street cars, based simply on race and color, is un-American, undemocratic and silly. We protest against all such discrimination.

Third. We claim the right of freemen to walk, talk and be with them who wish to be with us. No man has a right to choose another man's friends, and to attempt to do so is an impudent interference with the most fundamental human privilege.

Fourth. We want the laws enforced against rich as well as poor; against Capitalist as well as Laborer; against white as well as black. We are not more lawless than the white race; we are more often arrested, convicted and mobbed. We want justice even for criminals and outlaws. We want the Constitution of the country enforced. We want Congress to take charge of the Congressional elections. We want the Fourteenth Amendment carried out to the letter and every State disfranchised in Congress which attempts to disfranchise its rightful voters. We want the Fifteenth Amendment enforced and no State allowed to base its franchise simply on color.

The failure of the Republican Party in Congress at the session just closed to redeem its pledge of 1904 with reference to suffrage conditions in the South seems a plain, deliberate, and premeditated breach of promise, and stamps that party as guilty of obtaining votes under false pretense.

Fifth. We want our children educated. The school system in

the country districts of the South is a disgrace and in few towns and cities are the Negro schools what they ought to be. We want the national government to step in and wipe out illiteracy in the South. Either the United States will destroy ignorance, or ignorance will destroy the United States.

And when we call for education, we mean real education. We believe in work. We ourselves are workers, but work is not necessarily education. Education is the development of power and ideal. We want our children trained as intelligent human beings should be and we will fight for all time against any proposal to educate black boys and girls simply as servants and underlings, or simply for the use of other people. They have a right to know, to think, to aspire.

These are some of the chief things which we want. How shall we get them? By voting where we may vote; by persistent, unceasing agitation; by hammering at the truth; by sacrifice and work.

We do not believe in violence, neither in the despised violence of the raid nor the lauded violence of the soldier, not the barbarous violence of the mob; but we do believe in John Brown, in that incarnate spirit of justice, that hatred of a lie, that willingness to sacrifice money, reputation, and life itself on the altar of right. And here on the scene of John Brown's martyrdom, we reconsecrate ourselves, our honor, our property to the final emancipation of the race which John Brown died to make free.

FOR DISCUSSION

1. DuBois's speech was delivered in 1906. Explain why you believe it is or is not old-fashioned.
2. This selection seems to be a rebuttal of the ideas expressed in Booker T. Washington's speech. Contrast DuBois's ideas with those presented in the preceding selection by Booker T. Washington. Which author do you find more convincing? Why?

Black Identity

Dick Gregory

(*1932–*)

Comedian, actor, author, and civil rights leader, Dick Gregory achieved success despite hardships encountered in childhood. He was born in St. Louis, one of six children, whose father deserted them when Gregory was only five. He grew up on relief and watched his mother struggle to hold her family together by working for white families. She gave Gregory advice as a child which he has always followed: "Learn to live, not just make a living." Gregory became class president in high school when, according to him, he organized all "the so-called hoodlums. All those poor cats who, like me had been on the outside of everything." He won a scholarship to Illinois University. Later he began his night club performances as a comic and became the first black social satirist. Gregory has said "It's not just the white man, it's the black man who is racist too." He believes that we are "not in a battle between black and white; the real battle is between right and wrong."

Gregory's commitment to the civil rights movment has intensified in recent years, and he has given up numerous profitable night club engagements to tour college campuses and to organize demonstrations. He traveled the South in support of desegregation despite threats to his life. Also a pacifist, he staged a forty-day fast to protest the war in Vietnam. The following selection is taken from Gregory's autobiography, *Nigger*.

Not Poor, Just Broke

Like a lot of Negro kids, we never would have made it without our Momma. When there was no fatback to go with the beans, no socks to go with the shoes, no hope to go with tomorrow, she'd smile and say: "We ain't poor; we're just broke." Poor is a state of mind you never grow out of, but being broke is just a temporary condition. She always had a big smile, even when her legs and feet swelled from high blood pressure and she collapsed across the table with sugar diabetes. You have to smile twenty-four hours a day, Momma would say. If you walk through life showing the aggravation you've gone through, people will feel sorry for you, and they'll never respect you. She taught us that man has two ways out in life — laughing or crying. There's more hope in laughing. A man can fall down the stairs and lie there in such pain and horror that his own wife will collapse and faint at the sight. But if he can just hold back his pain for a minute she might be able to collect herself and call the doctor. It might mean the difference between his living to laugh again or dying there on the spot.

So you laugh; so you smile. Once a month the big gray relief truck would pull up in front of our house and Momma would flash that big smile and stretch out her hands. "Who else you know in this neighborhood gets this kind of service?" And we could all feel proud when the neighbors, folks who weren't on relief, folks who had Daddies in their houses, would come by the back porch for some of those hundred pounds of potatoes, for some sugar and flour and salty fish. We'd stand out there on the back porch and hand out the food like we were in charge of helping poor people, and then we'd take the food they brought us in return.

And Momma came home one hot summer day and found we'd been evicted, thrown out into the streetcar zone with our orange-crate chairs and secondhand lamps. She flashed that big smile and dried our tears and bought some penny Kool-Aid. We stood out there and sold drinks to thirsty people coming off the streetcar, and we thought nobody knew we were kicked out — figured they thought we *wanted* to be there. And Momma went off to talk the landlord into letting us back in on credit.

But I wonder about my Momma sometimes, and all the other Negro mothers who got up at 6 A.M. to go to the white man's house with sacks over their shoes because it was so wet and cold. I wonder how they made it. They worked very hard for the man, they made his breakfast, and they scrubbed his floors and they diapered his babies. They didn't have too much time for us.

I wonder about my Momma, who walked out of a white woman's clean house at midnight and came back to her own where the lights had been out for three months, and the pipes were frozen, and the wind came in through the cracks. She'd have to make deals with the rats: leave some food out for them so they wouldn't gnaw on the doors or bite the babies. The roaches, they were just like part of the family.

I wonder how she felt telling those white kids she took care of to brush their teeth after they ate, to wash their hands after they peed. She could never tell her own kids because there wasn't soap or water back home.

I wonder how my Momma felt when we came home from school with a list of vitamins and pills and cod liver oils the school nurse said we had to have. Momma would cry all night, and then go out and spend most of the rent money for pills. A week later, the white man would come for his eighteen dollars rent and Momma would plead with him to wait until tomorrow. She had lost her pocketbook. The relief check was coming. The white folks had some money for her. Tomorrow. I'd be hiding in the coal closet because there was only supposed to be two kids in the flat, and I could hear the rent man curse my Momma and call her a liar. And when he finally went away, Momma put the sacks on her shoes and went off to the rich white folks' house to dress the rich white kids so their mother could take them to a special baby doctor.

Momma had to take us to Homer G. Phillips, the free hospital, the city hospital for Negroes. We'd stand in line and wait for hours, smiling and Uncle Tomming every time a doctor or a nurse passed by. We'd feel good when one of them smiled back and didn't look at us as though we were dirty and had no right coming down there. All the doctors and nurses at Homer G. Phillips were Negro, too.

I remember one time when a doctor in white walked up and said: "What's wrong with him?" as if he didn't believe that anythings was.

Momma looked at me and looked at him and shook her head. "I sure don't know, Doctor, but he cried all night long. Held his stomach."

"Bring him in and get his damned clothes off."

I was so mad the way he was talking to my Momma that I bit down too hard on the thermometer. It broke in my mouth. The doctor slapped me across my face.

"Both of you go stand in the back of the line and wait your turn."

My Momma had to say: "I'm sorry, Doctor," and go to the back of the line. She had five other kids at home and she never knew when she'd have to bring another down to the City Hospital.

And those rich white folks Momma was so proud of. She'd sit around with the other women and they'd talk about how good their white folks were. They'd lie about how rich they were, what nice parties they gave, what good clothes they wore. And how they were going to be remembered in their white folks' wills. The next morning the white lady would say, "We're going on vacation for two months, Lucille; we won't be needing you until we get back." Damn. Two-month vacation without pay.

I wonder how my Momma stayed so good and beautiful in her soul when she worked seven days a week on swollen legs and feet, how she kept teaching us to smile and laugh when the house was dark and cold and she never knew when one of her hungry kids was going to ask about Daddy.

I wonder how she kept from teaching us hate when the social worker came around. She was a nasty woman with a pinched face who said, "We have reason to suspect you are working, Miss

Gregory, and you can be sure I'm going to check on you. We don't stand for welfare cheaters."

Momma, a welfare cheater. A criminal who couldn't stand to see her kids go hungry, or grow up in slums and end up mugging people in dark corners. I guess the system didn't want her to get off relief, the way it kept sending social workers around to be sure Momma wasn't trying to make things better.

I remember how that social worker would poke around the house, wrinkling her nose at the coal dust on the chilly linoleum floor, shaking her head at the bugs crawling over the dirty dishes in the sink. My Momma would have to stand there and make like she was too lazy to keep her own house clean. She could never let on that she spent all day cleaning another woman's house for two dollars and carfare. She would have to follow that nasty woman around those drafty three rooms, keeping her fingers crossed that the telephone hidden in the closet wouldn't ring. Welfare cases weren't supposed to have telephones.

But Momma figured that some day the Gregory kids were going to get off North Taylor Street and into a world where they would have to compete with kids who grew up with telephones in their houses. She didn't want us to be at a disadvantage. She couldn't explain that to the social worker. And she couldn't explain that while she was out spoon-feeding somebody else's kids, she was worrying about her own kids, that she could rest her mind by picking up the telephone and calling us — to find out if we had bread for our baloney or baloney for our bread, to see if any of us had gotten run over by the streetcar while we played in the gutter, to make sure the house hadn't burnt down from the papers and magazines we stuffed in the stove when the coal ran out.

But sometimes when she called there would be no answer. Home was a place to be only when all other places were closed.

I never learned hate at home, or shame. I had to go to school for that. I was about seven years old when I got my first big lesson. I was in love with a little girl named Helene Tucker, a light-complected little girl with pigtails and nice manners. She was always clean and she was smart in school. I think I went to school then mostly to look at her. I brushed my hair and even got me a little old handkerchief. It was a lady's handkerchief, but I didn't want Helene to see me wipe my nose on my hand. The pipes were frozen again; there was no water in the house, but I washed my socks and shirt every night. I'd get a pot, and go over to Mister Ben's grocery store, and stick my pot down into his soda machine. Scoop out some chopped ice. By evening the ice melted to water for washing. I got sick a lot that winter because the fire would go out at night before the clothes were dry. In the morning I'd put them on, wet or dry, because they were the only clothes I had.

Everybody's got a Helene Tucker, a symbol of everything you want. I loved her for her goodness, her cleanness, her popularity. She'd walk down my street and my brothers and sisters would yell, "Here comes Helene," and I'd rub my tennis sneakers on the back of my pants and wish my hair wasn't so nappy and the white folks' shirt fit me better. I'd run out on the street. If I knew my place and didn't come too close, she'd wink at me and say hello. That was a good feeling. Sometimes I'd follow her all the way home, and shovel the snow off her walk and try to make friends with her Momma and her aunts. I'd drop money on her stoop late at night on my way back from shining shoes in the taverns. And she had a Daddy, and he had a good job. He was a paper hanger.

I guess I would have gotten over Helene by summertime, but something happened in that classroom that made her face hang in front of me for the next twenty-two years. When I played the drums in high school it was for Helene, and when I broke track records in college, it was for Helene, and when I started standing behind microphones and heard applause I wished Helene could hear it, too. It wasn't until I was twenty-nine years old and married and making money that I finally got her out of my system. Helene was sitting in that classroom when I learned to be ashamed of myself.

It was on a Thursday. I was sitting in the back of the room, in a seat with a chalk circle drawn around it. The idiot's seat, the troublemaker's seat.

The teacher thought I was stupid. Couldn't spell, couldn't read, couldn't do arithmetic. Just stupid. Teachers were never interested in finding out that you couldn't concentrate because you were so hungry, because you hadn't had any breakfast. All you could think about was noontime; would it ever come? Maybe you could sneak into the cloakroom and steal a bite of some kid's lunch out of a coat pocket. A bite of something. Paste. You can't really make a meal of paste, or put it on bread for a sandwich, but sometimes I'd scoop a few spoonfuls out of the paste jar in the back of the room. Pregnant people get strange tastes. I was pregnant with poverty. Pregnant with dirt and pregnant with smells that made people turn away, pregnant with cold and pregnant with shoes that were never bought for me, pregnant with five other people in my bed and no Daddy in the next room, and pregnant with hunger. Paste doesn't taste too bad when you're hungry.

The teacher thought I was a troublemaker. All she saw from the front of the room was a little black boy who squirmed in his idiot's seat and made noises and poked the kids around him. I guess she couldn't see a kid who made noises because he wanted someone to know he was there.

It was on a Thursday, the day before the Negro payday. The eagle always flew on Friday. The teacher was asking each student how much his father would give to the Community Chest. On Friday night, each kid would get the money from his father, and on Monday he would bring it to the school. I decided I was going to buy me a Daddy right then. I had money in my pocket from shining shoes and selling papers, and whatever Helene Tucker pledged for her Daddy I was going to top it. And I'd hand the money right in. I wasn't going to wait until Monday to buy me a Daddy.

I was shaking, scared to death. The teacher opened her book and started calling out names alphabetically.

"Helene Tucker?"

"My Daddy said he'd give two dollars and fifty cents."

"That's very nice, Helene. Very, very nice indeed."

That made me feel pretty good. It wouldn't take too much to top that. I had almost three dollars in dimes and quarters in my pocket. I stuck my hand in my pocket and held onto the money, waiting for her to call my name. But the teacher closed her book after she called everybody else in the class.

I stood up and raised my hand.

"What is it now?"

"You forgot me."

She turned toward the blackboard. "I don't have time to be

playing with you, Richard."

"My Daddy said he'd. . . ."

"Sit down, Richard; you're disturbing the class."

"My Daddy said he'd give . . . fifteen dollars."

She turned around and looked mad. "We are collecting this money for you and your kind, Richard Gregory. If your Daddy can give fifteen dollars you have no business being on relief."

"I got it right now, I got it right now, my Daddy gave it to me to turn in today, my Daddy said. . . ."

"And furthermore," she said, looking right at me, her nostrils getting big and her lips getting thin and her eyes opening wide, "we know you don't have a Daddy."

Helene Tucker turned around, her eyes full of tears. She felt sorry for me. Then I couldn't see her too well because I was crying, too.

"Sit down, Richard."

And I always thought the teacher kind of liked me. She always picked me to wash the blackboard on Friday, after school. That was a big thrill; it made me feel important. If I didn't wash it, come Monday the school might not function right.

"Where are you going, Richard?"

I walked out of school that day, and for a long time I didn't go back very often. There was shame there.

Now there was shame everywhere. It seemed like the whole world had been inside that classroom; everyone had heard what the teacher had said; everyone had turned around and felt sorry for me. There was shame in going to the Worthy Boys' Annual Christmas Dinner for you and your kind, because everybody knew what a worthy boy was. Why couldn't they just call it the Boys' Annual Dinner; why'd they have to give it a name? There was shame in wearing the brown and orange and white plaid mackinaw the welfare gave to 3,000 boys. Why'd it have to be the same for everybody so when you walked down the street the people could see you were on relief? It was a nice warm mackinaw and it had a hood, and my Momma beat me and called me a little rat when she found out I stuffed it in the bottom of a pail full of garbage way over on Cottage Street. There was shame in running over to Mister Ben's at the end of the day and asking for his rotten peaches; there was shame in asking Mrs. Simmons for a spoonful of sugar; there was shame in running out to meet the relief truck. I hated that truck, full of food for you and your kind. I ran into the house and hid when it came. And then I started to sneak through alleys, to take the long way home so the people going into White's Eat Shop wouldn't see me. Yeah, the whole world heard the teacher that day; we all know you don't have a Daddy.

It lasted for a while, this kind of numbness. I spent a lot of time feeling sorry for myself. And then one day I met this wino in a restaurant. I'd been out hustling all day, shining shoes, selling newspapers, and I had googobs of money in my pocket. Bought me a bowl of chili for fifteen cents, and a cheeseburger for fifteen cents, and a Pepsi for five cents, and a piece of chocolate cake for ten cents. That was a good meal. I was eating when this old wino came in. I love winos because they never hurt anyone but themselves.

The old wino sat down at the counter and ordered twenty-six cents worth of food. He ate it like he really enjoyed it. When the owner, Mister Williams, asked him to pay the check, the old wino didn't lie or go through his pocket like he suddenly found a hole.

He just said, "Don't have no money."

The owner yelled, "Why in hell you come in here and eat my food if you don't have no money? That food cost me money."

Mister Williams jumped over the counter and knocked the wino off his stool and beat him over the head with a pop bottle. Then he stepped back and watched the wino bleed. Then he kicked him. And he kicked him again.

I looked at the wino with blood all over his face and I went over. "Leave him alone, Mister Williams. I'll pay the twenty-six cents."

The wino got up, slowly, pulling himself up to the stool, then up to the counter, holding on for a minute until his legs stopped shaking so bad. He looked at me with pure hate. "Keep your twenty-six cents. You don't have to pay, not now. I just finished paying for it."

He started to walk out, and as he passed me, he reached down and touched my shoulder. "Thanks, sonny, but it's too late now. Why didn't you pay it before?"

I was pretty sick about that. I waited too long to help another man.

I remember a white lady who came to our door once around Thanksgiving time. She wore a woolly, green bonnet around her head, and she smiled a lot.

"Is your mother home, little boy?"

"No, she ain't."

"May I come in?"

"What do you want, ma'am?"

She didn't stop smiling once, but she sighed a little when she bent down and lifted up a big yellow basket. The kind I saw around church that were called Baskets for the Needy.

"This is for you."

"What's in there?"

"All sorts of good things," she said, smiling. "There's candy and potatoes and cake and cranberry sauce and" — she made a funny little face at me by wrinkling up her nose — "and a great big fat turkey for Thanksgiving dinner."

"Is it cooked?"

"A big fat juicy turkey, all plucked clean for you. . . ."

"Is it cooked?"

"No, it's not. . . ."

"We ain't got nothing in the house to cook it with, lady."

I slammed the door in her face. Wouldn't that be something, to have a turkey like that in the house with no way to cook it? No gas, no electricity, no coal. Just a big fat juicy raw turkey.

I remember Mister Ben, the grocery-store man, a round little white man with funny little tufts of white hair on his head and sad-looking eyes. His face was kind of gray-colored, and the skin was loose and shook when he talked.

"Momma want a loaf of bread, Mister Ben, fresh bread."

"Right away, Richard," he'd say and get the bread he bought three days old from the bakeries downtown. It was the only kind he had for his credit-book customers. He dropped it on the counter. Clunk.

I'd hand him the credit book, that green tablet with the picture of the snuff can on it, to write down how much we owed him. He'd lick the tip of that stubby pencil he kept behind his ear. Six cents.

"How you like school, Richard?"

"I like school fine, Mister Ben."

"Good boy, you study, get smart."

I'd run home to Momma and tell her that the bread wasn't fresh bread, it was stale bread. She'd flash the big smile.

"Oh, that Mister Ben, he knew I was fixin to make toast."

The peaches were rotten and the bread wasn't fresh and sometimes the butter was green, but when it came down to the nitty-gritty you could always go to Mister Ben. Before a Jewish holiday he'd take all the food that was going to spoil while the store was shut and bring it over to our house. Before Christmas he'd send over some meat even though he knew it was going on the tablet and he might never see his money. When the push came to the shove and every hungry belly in the house was beginning to eat on itself, Momma could go to Mister Ben and always get enough for some kind of dinner.

But I can remember three days in a row I went into Mister Ben's and asked him to give me a penny Mr. Goodbar from the window.

Three days in a row he said: "Out, out, or I'll tell your Momma you been begging."

One night I threw a brick through his window and took it.

The next day I went into Mister Ben's to get some bread for Momma and his skin was shaking and I heard him tell a lady, "I can't understand why should anybody break my window for a penny piece of candy, a lousy piece of candy, all they got to do is ask, that's all, and I give."

FOR DISCUSSION

1. Describe Gregory's teacher. What happens to Gregory at school? From your experience, how common are such situations?
2. Compare the attitudes of the different white people in this selection toward Gregory and his family. Which, if any, of the white characters are favorably portrayed?

Malcolm X
(1925–1965)

Malcolm X lived in Michigan until his father died and his mother was committed to a mental hospital. Sent to live with a sister in Roxbury, Massachusetts, he sold marijuana and became a thief. "In the society to which I was exposed as a black youth here in America," he later commented, "for me to wind up in a prison was just about inevitable." He was eventually sentenced to ten years in Charlestown State Prison for burglary. After his release, he met Elijah Muhammad, leader of the Black Muslims. Questioning how, in American society, there can "ever be any white-black solidarity before there is first some black solidarity," Malcolm X became one of the primary leaders of the Black Muslim movement. After visiting Africa he modified his position. He broke with the Muslims and formed the Organization of Afro-American Unity, a non-religious group concentrated upon political action.

Malcolm X once remarked: "I believe that it would be almost impossible to find anywhere in America a black man who has lived further down in the mud of human society than I have; or a black man who has been any more ignorant than I have been; or a black man who has suffered more anguish during his life than I have. But it is only after the deepest darkness that the greatest joy can come; it is only after slavery and prison that the sweetest appreciation of freedom can come." The thirty-nine year old leader was murdered in Harlem in 1965.

Mascot

FROM *The Autobiography of Malcolm X*

They told me I was going to go to a reform school. I was still thirteen years old.

But first I was going to the detention home. It was in Mason, Michigan, about twelve miles from Lansing. The detention home was where all the "bad" boys and girls from Ingham County were held, on their way to reform school — waiting for their hearings.

The white state man was a Mr. Maynard Allen. He was nicer to me than most of the state Welfare people had been. He even had consoling words for the Gohannases and Mrs. Adcock and Big Boy; all of them were crying. But I wasn't. With the few clothes I owned stuffed into a box, we rode in his car to Mason. He talked as he drove along, saying that my school marks showed that if I would just straighten up, I could make something of myself. He said that reform school had the wrong reputation; he talked about what the word "reform" meant — to change and become better. He said the school was really a place where boys like me could have time to see their mistakes and start a new life and become somebody everyone would be proud of. And he told me that the lady in charge of the detention home, a Mrs. Swerlin, and her husband were very good people.

They were good people. Mrs. Swerlin was bigger than her husband, I remember, a big, buxom, robust, laughing woman, and Mr. Swerlin was thin, with black hair, and a black mustache and a red face, quiet and polite, even to me.

They liked me right away, too. Mrs. Swerlin showed me to my room, my own room — the first in my life. It was in one of those huge dormitory-like buildings where kids in detention were kept

35

in those days — and still are in most places. I discovered next, with surprise, that I was allowed to eat with the Swerlins. It was the first time I'd eaten with white people — at least with grown white people — since the Seventh Day Adventist country meetings. It wasn't my own exclusive privilege, of course. Except for the very troublesome boys and girls at the detention home, who were kept locked up — those who had run away and been caught and brought back, or something like that — all of us ate with the Swerlins sitting at the head of the long tables.

They had a white cook-helper, I recall — Lucille Lathrop. (It amazes me how these names come back, from a time I haven't thought about for more than twenty years.) Lucille treated me well, too. Her husband's name was Duane Lathrop. He worked somewhere else, but he stayed there at the detention home on the weekends with Lucille.

I noticed again how white people smelled different from us, and how their food tasted different, not seasoned like Negro cooking. I began to sweep and mop and dust around in the Swerlins' house, as I had done with Big Boy at the Gohannases.

They all liked my attitude, and it was out of their liking for me that I soon became accepted by them — as a mascot, I know now. They would talk about anything and everything with me standing right there hearing them, the same way people would talk freely in front of a pet canary. They would even talk about me, or about "niggers," as though I wasn't there, as if I wouldn't understand what the word meant. A hundred times a day, they used the word "nigger." I suppose that in their own minds, they meant no harm; in fact they probably meant well. It was the same with the cook, Lucille, and her husband, Duane. I remember one day when Mr. Swerlin, as nice as he was, came in from Lansing, where he had been through the Negro section, and said to Mrs. Swerlin right in front of me, "I just can't see how those niggers can be so happy and be so poor." He talked about how they lived in shacks, but had those big, shining cars out front.

And Mrs. Swerlin said, me standing right there, "Niggers are just that way. . . ." That scene always stayed with me.

It was the same with the other white people, most of them local politicians, when they would come visiting the Swerlins. One of their favorite parlor topics was "niggers." One of them was the

judge who was in charge of me in Lansing. He was a close friend
of the Swerlins. He would ask about me when he came, and they
would call me in, and he would look me up and down, his expression approving, like he was examining a fine colt, or a pedigreed
pup. I knew they must have told him how I acted and how I
worked.

What I am trying to say is that it just never dawned upon them
that I could understand, that I wasn't a pet, but a human being.
They didn't give me credit for having the same sensitivity, intellect,
and understanding that they would have been ready and willing
to recognize in a white boy in my position. But it has historically
been the case with white people, in their regard for black people,
that even though we might be *with* them, we weren't considered
of them. Even though they appeared to have opened the door,
it was still closed. Thus they never did really see *me*.

This is the sort of kindly condescension which I try to clarify
today, to these integration-hungry Negroes, about their "liberal"
white friends, these so-called "good white people" — most of them
anyway. I don't care how nice one is to you; the thing you must
always remember is that almost never does he really see you as
he sees himself, as he sees his own kind. He may stand with
you through thin, but not thick; when the chips are down, you'll
find that as fixed in him as his bone structure is his sometimes
subconscious conviction that he's better than anybody black.

But I was no more than vaguely aware of anything like that
in my detention-home years. I did my little chores around the
house, and everything was fine. And each weekend, they didn't
mind my catching a ride over to Lansing for the afternoon or
evening. If I wasn't old enough, I sure was big enough by then,
and nobody ever questioned my hanging out, even at night, in
the streets of the Negro section.

I was growing up to be even bigger than Wilfred and Philbert,
who had begun to meet girls at the school dances, and other places,
and introduced me to a few. But the ones who seemed to like
me, I didn't go for — and vice versa. I couldn't dance a lick, anyway,
and I couldn't see squandering my few dimes on girls. So mostly
I pleasured myself these Saturday nights by gawking around the
Negro bars and restaurants. The jukeboxes were wailing Erskine
Hawkins's "Tuxedo Junction," Slim and Slam's "Flatfoot Floogie,"

things like that. Sometimes, big bands from New York, out touring the one-night stands in the sticks, would play for big dances in Lansing. Everybody with legs would come out to see any performer who bore the magic name "New York." Which is how I first heard Lucky Thompson and Milt Jackson, both of whom I later got to know well in Harlem.

Many youngsters from the detention home, when their dates came up, went off to the reform school. But when mine came up — two or three times — it was always ignored. I saw new youngsters arrive and leave. I was glad and grateful. I knew it was Mrs. Swerlin's doing. I didn't want to leave.

She finally told me one day that I was going to be entered in Mason Junior High School. It was the only school in town. No ward of the detention home had ever gone to school there, at least while still a ward. So I entered their seventh grade. The only other Negroes there were some of the Lyons children, younger than I was, in the lower grades. The Lyonses and I, as it happened, were the town's only Negroes. They were, as Negroes, very much respected. Mr. Lyons was a smart, hardworking man, and Mrs. Lyons was a very good woman. She and my mother, I had heard my mother say, were two of the four West Indians in that whole section of Michigan.

Some of the white kids at school, I found, were even friendlier than some of those in Lansing had been. Though some, including the teachers, called me "nigger," it was easy to see that they didn't mean any more harm by it than the Swerlins. As the "nigger" of my class, I was in fact extremely popular — I suppose partly because I was kind of a novelty. I was in demand; I had top priority. But I also benefited from the special prestige of having the seal of approval from that Very Important Woman about the town of Mason, Mrs. Swerlin. Nobody in Mason would have dreamed of getting on the wrong side of her. It became hard for me to get through a school day without someone after me to join this or head up that — the debating society, the Junior High basketball team, or some other extracurricular activity. I never turned them down.

And I hadn't been in the school long when Mrs. Swerlin, knowing I could use spending money of my own, got me a job after school washing the dishes in a local restaurant. My boss there was the father of a white classmate whom I spent a lot of time with. His family lived over the restaurant. It was fine working there. Every Friday night when I got paid, I'd feel at least ten feet tall. I forget how much I made, but it seemed like a lot. It was the first time I'd ever had any money to speak of, all my own, in my whole life. As soon as I could afford it, I bought a green suit and some shoes, and at school I'd buy treats for the others in my class — at least as much as any of them did for me.

English and history were the subjects I liked most. My English teacher, I recall — a Mr. Ostrowski — was always giving advice about how to become something in life. The one thing I didn't like about history class was that the teacher, Mr. Williams, was a great one for "nigger" jokes. One day during my first week at school, I walked into the room and he started singing to the class, as a joke, "Way down yonder in the cotton field, some folks say that a nigger won't steal." Very funny. I liked history, but I never thereafter had much liking for Mr. Williams. Later, I remember, we came to the textbook section on Negro history. It was exactly one paragraph long. Mr. Williams laughed through it practically in a single breath, reading aloud how the Negroes had been slaves and then were freed, and how they were usually lazy and dumb and shiftless. He added, I remember, an anthropological footnote on his own, telling us between laughs how Negroes' feet were "so big that when they walk, they don't leave tracks; they leave a hole in the ground."

I'm sorry to say that the subject I most disliked was mathematics. I have thought about it. I think the reason was that mathematics leaves no room for argument. It you made a mistake, that was all there was to it.

Basketball was a big thing in my life, though. I was on the team; we traveled to neighboring towns such as Howell and Charlotte, and wherever I showed my face, the audiences in the gymnasiums "niggered" and "cooned" me to death. Or called me "Rastus." It didn't bother my teammates or my coach at all, and to tell the truth, it bothered me only vaguely. Mine was the same psychology that makes Negroes even today, though it bothers them down inside, keep letting the white man tell them how much "progress" they are making. They've heard it so much they've almost gotten brainwashed into believing it — or at least accepting it.

After the basketball games, there would usually be a school

dance. Whenever our team walked into another school's gym for the dance, with me among them, I could feel the freeze. It would start to ease as they saw that I didn't try to mix, but stuck close to someone on our team, or kept to myself. I think I developed ways to do it without making it obvious. Even at our own school, I could sense it almost as a physical barrier, that despite all the beaming and smiling, the mascot wasn't supposed to dance with any of the white girls.

It was some kind of psychic message — not from them, but also from within myself. I am proud to be able to say that much for myself, at least. I would just stand around and smile and talk and drink punch and eat sandwiches, and then I would make some excuse and get away early.

They were typical small-town school dances. Sometimes a little white band from Lansing would be brought in to play. But most often, the music was a phonograph set up on a table, with the volume turned up high, and the records scratchy, blaring things like Glenn Miller's "Moonlight Serenade" — his band was riding high then — or the Ink Spots, who were also very popular, singing "If I Didn't Care."

I used to spend a lot of time thinking about a peculiar thing. Many of these Mason white boys, like the ones at the Lansing school — especially if they knew me well, and if we hung out a lot together — would get me off in a corner somewhere and push me to proposition certain white girls, sometimes their own sisters. They would tell me that they'd already had the girls themselves — including their sisters — or that they were trying to and couldn't. Later on, I came to understand what was going on: if they could get the girls into the position of having broken the terrible taboo by slipping off with me somewhere, they would have that hammer over the girls' heads, to make them give in to them.

It seemed that the white boys felt that I, being a Negro, just naturally knew more about "romance," or sex, than they did — that I instinctively knew more about what to do and say with their own girls. I never did tell anybody that I really went for some of the white girls, and some of them went for me, too. They let me know in many ways. But anytime we found ourselves in any close conversations or potentially intimate situations, always there would come up between us some kind of a wall. The girls I really wanted to have were a couple of Negro girls whom Wilfred or

Philbert had introduced me to in Lansing. But with these girls, somehow, I lacked the nerve.

From what I heard and saw on the Saturday nights I spent hanging around in the Negro district I knew that race-mixing went on in Lansing. But strangely enough, this didn't have any kind of effect on me. Every Negro in Lansing, I guess, knew how white men would drive along certain streets in the black neighborhoods and pick up Negro streetwalkers who patrolled the area. And, on the other hand, there was a bridge that separated the Negro and Polish neighborhoods, where white women would drive or walk across and pick up Negro men who would hang around in certain places close to the bridge, waiting for them. Lansing's white women, even in those days, were famous for chasing Negro men. I didn't yet appreciate how most whites accord to the Negro this reputation for prodigious sexual prowess. There in Lansing, I never heard of any trouble about this mixing, from either side. I imagine that everyone simply took it for granted, as I did.

Anyway, from my experience as a little boy at the Lansing school, I had become fairly adept at avoiding the white-girl issue — at least for a couple of years yet.

Then, in the second semester of the seventh grade, I was elected class president. It surprised me even more than other people. But I can see now why the class might have done it. My grades were among the highest in the school. I was unique in my class, like a pink poodle. And I was proud; I'm not going to say I wasn't. In fact, by then, I didn't really have much feeling about being a Negro, because I was trying so hard, in every way I could, to be white. Which is why I am spending much of my life today telling the American black man that he's wasting his time straining to "integrate." I know from personal experience. I tried hard enough.

"Malcolm, we're just so *proud* of you!" Mrs. Swerlin exclaimed when she heard about my election. It was all over the restaurant where I worked. Even the state man, Maynard Allen, who still dropped by to see me once in a while, had a word of praise. He said he never saw anybody prove better exactly what "reform" meant. I really liked him — except for one thing: he now and then would drop something that hinted my mother had let us down somehow.

Fairly often, I would go and visit the Lyonses, and they acted as happy as though I was one of their children. And it was the same warm feeling when I went into Lansing to visit my brothers and sisters, and the Gohannases.

I remember one thing that marred this time for me: the movie *Gone with the Wind.* When it played in Mason, I was the only Negro in the theater, and when Butterfly McQueen went into her act, I felt like crawling under the rug.

Every Saturday, just about, I would go into Lansing. I was going on fourteen, now. Wilfred and Hilda still lived out by themselves at the old family home. Hilda kept the house very clean. It was easier than my mother's plight, with eight of us always under foot or running around. Wilfred worked wherever he could, and he still read every book he could get his hands on. Philbert was getting a reputation as one of the better amateur fighters in this part of the state; everyone really expected that he was going to become a professional.

Reginald and I, after my fighting fiasco, had finally gotten back on good terms. It made me feel great to visit him and Wesley over at Mrs. Williams's. I'd offhandedly give them each a couple of dollars to just stick in their pockets, to have something to spend. And little Yvonne and Robert were doing okay, too, over at the home of the West Indian lady, Mrs. McGuire. I'd give them about a quarter apiece; it made me feel good to see how they were coming along.

None of us talked much about our mother. And we never mentioned our father. I guess none of us knew what to say. We didn't want anybody else to mention our mother either, I think. From time to time, though, we would all go over to Kalamazoo to visit her. Most often we older ones went singly, for it was something you didn't want to have to experience with anyone else present, even your brother or sister.

During this period, the visit to my mother that I most remember was toward the end of that seventh-grade year, when our father's grown daughter by his first marriage, Ella, came from Boston to visit us. Wilfred and Hilda had exchanged some letters with Ella, and I, at Hilda's suggestion, had written to her from the Swerlins'. We were all excited and happy when her letter told us that she was coming to Lansing.

I think the major impact of Ella's arrival, at least upon me, was that she was the first really proud black woman I had ever seen in my life. She was plainly proud of her very dark skin. This was unheard of among Negroes in those days, especially in Lansing.

I hadn't been sure just what day she would come. And then one afternoon I got home from school and there she was. She hugged me, stood me away, looked me up and down. A commanding woman, maybe even bigger than Mrs. Swerlin, Ella wasn't just black, but like our father, she was jet black. The way she sat, moved, talked, did everything, bespoke somebody who did and got exactly what she wanted. This was the woman my father had boasted of so often for having brought so many of their family out of Georgia to Boston. She owned some property, he would say, and she was "in society." She had come North with nothing, and she had worked and saved and had invested in property that she built up in value, and then she started sending money to Georgia for another sister, brother, cousin, niece, or nephew to come north to Boston. All that I had heard was reflected in Ella's appearance and bearing. I had never been so impressed with anybody. She was in her second marriage; her first husband had been a doctor.

Ella asked all kinds of questions about how I was doing; she had already heard from Wilfred and Hilda about my election as class president. She asked especially about my grades, and I ran and got my report cards. I was then one of the three highest in the class. Ella praised me. I asked her about her brother, Earl, and her sister, Mary. She had the exciting news that Earl was a singer with a band in Boston. He was singing under the name of Jimmy Carleton. Mary was also doing well.

Ella told me about other relatives from that branch of the family. A number of them I'd never heard of; she had helped them up from Georgia. They, in their turn, had helped up others. "We Littles have to stick together," Ella said. It thrilled me to hear her say that, and even more, the way she said it. I had become a mascot; our branch of the family was split to pieces; I had just about forgotten about being a Little in any family sense. She said that different members of the family were working in good jobs, and some even had small businesses going. Most of them were homeowners.

When Ella suggested that all of us Littles in Lansing accompany her on a visit to our mother, we all were grateful. We all felt that if anyone could do anything that could help our mother, that might help her get well and come back, it would be Ella. Anyway, all of us, for the first time together, went with Ella to Kalamazoo.

Our mother was smiling when they brought her out. She was extremely surprised when she saw Ella. They made a striking contrast, the thin near-white woman and the big black one hugging each other. I don't remember much about the rest of the visit, except that there was a lot of talking, and Ella had everything in hand, and we left with all of us feeling better than we ever had about the circumstances. I know that for the first time, I felt as though I had visited with someone who had some kind of physical illness that had just lingered on.

A few days later, after visiting the homes where each of us were staying, Ella left Lansing and returned to Boston. But before leaving, she told me to write to her regularly. And she had suggested that I might like to spend my summer holiday visiting her in Boston. I jumped at that chance.

That summer of 1940, in Lansing, I caught the Greyhound bus for Boston with my cardboard suitcase, and wearing my green suit. If someone had hung a sign, "HICK," around my neck, I couldn't have looked much more obvious. They didn't have the turnpikes then; the bus stopped at what seemed every corner and cowpatch. From my seat in — you guessed it — the back of the bus, I gawked out of the window at white man's America rolling past for what seemed a month, but must have been only a day and a half.

When we finally arrived, Ella met me at the terminal and took me home. The house was on Waumbeck Street in the Sugar Hill section of Roxbury, the Harlem of Boston. I met Ella's second husband, Frank, who was now a soldier; and her brother Earl, the singer who called himself Jimmy Carleton; and Mary, who was very different from her older sister. It's funny how I seemed to think of Mary as Ella's sister, instead of her being, just as Ella is, my own half sister. It's probably because Ella and I always were much closer as basic types; we're dominant people, and Mary has always been mild and quiet, almost shy.

Ella was busily involved in dozens of things. She belonged to I don't know how many different clubs; she was a leading light of local so-called "black society." I saw and met a hundred black people there whose big-city talk and ways left my mouth hanging open.

I couldn't have feigned indifference if I had tried to. People talked casually about Chicago, Detroit, New York. I didn't know the world contained as many Negroes as I saw thronging downtown Roxbury at night, especially on Saturdays. Neon lights, nightclubs, poolhalls, bars, the cars they drove! Restaurants made the streets smell — rich, greasy, down-home black cooking! Jukeboxes blared Erskine Hawkins, Duke Ellington, Cootie Williams, dozens of others. If somebody had told me then that some day I'd know them all personally, I'd have found it hard to believe. The biggest bands, like these, played at the Roseland State Ballroom, on Boston's Massachusetts Avenue — one night for Negroes, the next night for whites.

I saw for the first time occasional black-white couples strolling around arm in arm. And on Sundays, when Ella, Mary, or somebody took me to church, I saw churches for black people such as I had never seen. They were many times finer than the white church I had attended back in Mason, Michigan. There, the white people just sat and worshiped with words; but the Boston Negroes, like all other Negroes I had ever seen at church, threw their souls and bodies wholly into worship.

Two or three times, I wrote letters to Wilfred intended for everybody back in Lansing. I said I'd try to describe it when I got back.

But I found I couldn't.

My restlessness with Mason — and for the first time in my life a restlessness with being around white people — began as soon as I got back home and entered eighth grade.

I continued to think constantly about all that I had seen in Boston, and about the way I had felt there. I know now that it was the sense of being a real part of a mass of my own kind, for the first time.

The white people — classmates, the Swerlins, the people at the restaurant where I worked — noticed the change. They said, "You're acting so strange. You don't seem like yourself, Malcolm. What's the matter?"

I kept close to the top of the class, though. The topmost scholastic standing, I remember, kept shifting between me, a girl named

Audrey Slaugh, and a boy named Jimmy Cotton.

It went on that way, as I became increasingly restless and disturbed through the first semester. And then one day, just about when those of us who had passed were about to move up to 8-A, from which we would enter high school the next year, something happened which was to become the first major turning point of my life.

Somehow, I happened to be alone in the classroom with Mr. Ostrowski, my English teacher. He was a tall, rather reddish white man and he had a thick mustache. I had gotten some of my best marks under him, and he had always made me feel that he liked me. He was, as I have mentioned, a natural-born "advisor," about what you ought to read, to do, or think — about any and everything. We used to make unkind jokes about him: why was he teaching in Mason instead of somewhere else, getting for himself some of the "success in life" that he kept telling us how to get?

I know that he probably meant well in what he happened to advise me that day. I doubt that he meant any harm. It was just in his nature as an American white man. I was one of his top students, one of the school's top students — but all he could see for me was the kind of future "in your place" that almost all white people see for black people.

He told me, "Malcolm, you ought to be thinking about a career. Have you been giving it thought?"

The truth is, I hadn't. I never have figured out why I told him, "Well, yes, sir, I've been thinking I'd like to be a lawyer." Lansing certainly had no Negro lawyers — or doctors either — in those days, to hold up an image I might have aspired to. All I really knew for certain was that a lawyer didn't wash dishes, as I was doing.

Mr. Ostrowski looked surprised, I remember, and leaned back in his chair and clasped his hands behind his head. He kind of half-smiled and said, "Malcolm, one of life's first needs is for us to be realistic. Don't misunderstand me, now. We all here like you, you know that. But you've got to be realistic about being a nigger. A lawyer — that's no realistic goal for a nigger. You need to think about something you *can* be. You're good with your hands — making things. Everybody admires your carpentry shop work. Why don't you plan on carpentry? People like you as a person — you'd get all kinds of work."

The more I thought afterwards about what he said, the more uneasy it made me. It just kept treading around in my mind.

What made it really begin to disturb me was Mr. Ostrowski's advice to others in my class — all of them white. Most of them had told him they were planning to become farmers. But those who wanted to strike out on their own, to try something new, he had encouraged. Some, mostly girls, wanted to be teachers. A few wanted other professions, such as one boy who wanted to become a county agent; another, a veterinarian; and one girl wanted to be a nurse. They all reported that Mr. Ostrowski had encouraged what they had wanted. Yet nearly none of them had earned marks equal to mine.

It was a surprising thing that I had never thought of it that way before, but I realized that whatever I wasn't, I *was* smarter than nearly all of those white kids. But apparently I was still not intelligent enough, in their eyes, to become whatever *I* wanted to be.

It was then that I began to change — inside.

I drew away from white people. I came to class, and I answered when called upon. It became a physical strain simply to sit in Mr. Ostrowski's class.

Where "nigger" had slipped off my back before, wherever I heard it now, I stopped and looked at whoever said it. And they looked surprised that I did.

I quit hearing so much "nigger" and "What's wrong?" — which was the way I wanted it. Nobody, including the teachers, could decide what had come over me. I knew I was being discussed.

In a few more weeks, it was that way, too, at the restaurant where I worked washing dishes, and at the Swerlins'.

One day soon after, Mrs. Swerlin called me into the living room, and there was the state man, Maynard Allen. I knew from their faces that something was about to happen. She told me that none of them could understand why — after I had done so well in school, and on my job, and living with them, and after everyone in Mason had come to like me — I had lately begun to make them all feel that I wasn't happy there anymore.

She said she felt there was no need for me to stay at the detention home any longer, and that arrangements had been made for me to go and live with the Lyons family, who liked me so much.

She stood up and put out her hand. "I guess I've asked you a hundred times, Malcolm — do you want to tell me what's wrong?"

I shook her hand, and said, "Nothing, Mrs. Swerlin." Then I went and got my things, and came back down. At the living room door I saw her wiping her eyes. I felt very bad. I thanked her and went out in front to Mr. Allen, who took me over to the Lyonses'.

Mr. and Mrs. Lyons, and their children, during the two months I lived with them — while finishing eighth grade — also tried to get me to tell them what was wrong. But somehow I couldn't tell them, either.

I went every Saturday to see my brothers and sisters in Lansing, and almost every other day I wrote to Ella in Boston. Not saying why, I told Ella that I wanted to come there and live.

I don't know how she did it, but she arranged for official custody of me to be transferred from Michigan to Massachusetts, and the very week I finished the eighth grade, I again boarded the Greyhound bus for Boston.

I've thought about that time a lot since then. No physical move in my life has been more pivotal or profound in its repercussions.

If I had stayed on in Michigan, I would probably have married one of those Negro girls I knew and liked in Lansing. I might have become one of those state capitol building shoeshine boys, or a Lansing Country Club waiter, or gotten one of the other menial jobs which, in those days, among Lansing Negroes, would have been considered "successful" — or even become a carpenter.

Whatever I have done since then, I have driven myself to become a success at it. I've often thought that if Mr. Ostrowski had encouraged me to become a lawyer, I would today probably be among some city's professional black bourgeoisie, sipping cocktails and palming myself off as a community spokesman for and leader of the suffering black masses, while my primary concern would be to grab a few more crumbs from the groaning board of the two-faced whites with whom they're begging to "integrate."

All praise is due to Allah that I went to Boston when I did. If I hadn't, I'd probably still be a brainwashed black Christian.

FOR DISCUSSION

1. Malcolm X says that blacks should always be suspicious of whites because as fixed in the white man "as his bone structure is his . . . conviction that he's better than anybody black." Explain why you agree or disagree with this statement.

2. Although Malcolm X was an outstanding student, Mr. Ostrowski, his seventh-grade English teacher, tells him to be "realistic about being a nigger. A lawyer — that's no realistic goal for a nigger." How is this incident useful in evaluating Booker T. Washington's ideas in his Atlanta speech, "Cast Down Your Bucket . . ."?

Claude Brown

(1937–   )

Brought up in Harlem, Claude Brown learned at an early age how to survive in the streets. He soon joined a Harlem gang and gained "a sort of social status" by stealing. At age eleven, Brown was sent to the Wiltwyck School for emotionally disturbed and deprived boys and encountered his lifetime friend, Dr. Ernest Papanek. When he returned to the streets, Brown began to sell and use marijuana, and at fourteen he was sent to Warwick reform school. In 1953, he received his final release from Warwick and became a "hustler" in drugs; fortunately, he never became an addict. At sixteen, Brown began night courses at Washington Irving High School and his long climb out of the ghetto. On a grant from the Metropolitan Community Methodist Church, he went to Howard University. During his first year there, Papanek urged him to write an article on life in Harlem for *Dissent* magazine, and it was this article which called attention to his writing talent. He completed the manuscript for *Manchild in the Promised Land* on a Macmillan expense account and established himself with its publication as an authoritative voice for black America. "I'm trying to show more than anything else the humanity of the Negro," says Brown. "Somebody has to stop problemizing and start humanizing the Negro."

FROM

Manchild in the Promised Land

Mama and Dad were going to try to guide us and make us do right and be good, and they didn't even know what being good was. When I was a little boy, Mama and Dad would beat me and tell me, "You better be good," but I didn't know what being good was. To me, it meant that they just wanted me to sit down and fold my hands or something crazy like that. Stay in front of the house, don't go anyplace, don't get into trouble. I didn't know what it meant, and I don't think they knew what it meant, because they couldn't ever tell me what they really wanted. The way I saw it, everything I was doing was good. If I stole something and didn't get caught, I was good. If I got into a fight with somebody, I tried to be good enough to beat him. If I broke into a place, I tried to be quiet and steal as much as I could. I was always trying to be good. They just kept on beating me and talking about being good. And I just kept on doing what I was doing and kept on trying to do it good.

They needed some help. The way I felt about it, I should have been their parents, because I had been out there on the streets, and I wasn't as far back in the woods as they were. I could have told them a whole lot of stuff that would have helped them, Mama and Dad and Papa, everybody, if they had only listened to me.

I remember how Dad thought being a busboy was a real good job. When I was working at Hamburger Heaven, I stayed there for a year, and I don't know how I did it. I was working for nine hours a day, six days a week, and going to school at night. He still felt that this was a good job, because he'd never made any

51

money. He'd never made more than sixty dollars a week in his life until recently. I suppose when he was my age, he was only making something like thirty dollars a week and thought it was a whole lot of money. He figured if I was making forty-five dollars a week, that was a whole lot of money. The cat was crazy. I would spend forty-five dollars on a pair of shoes. To him it was a good job because when he was nine years old, he'd plowed the fields from sunup to sundown.

I came in one night and told Mama. I said, "Mama, I'm gon quit this job at Hamburger Heaven, because it's getting too damn hard on me."

Dad was sitting over in the corner in his favorite chair reading the newspaper. He wouldn't look up, because we could never talk. We just never talked too much after we had our last fight.

I said I was going to school, and that plus the job was kind of rough on me.

After Dad couldn't take any more, he lifted his head out of the paper and said, "Boy, you don't need all that education. You better keep that job, because that's a good job."

"Yeah, Dad, it's good as long as you can take it, but if it kills you, there's nothing good about that."

He said, "Hard work ain't never killed nobody, unless they was so lazy that thinkin' about it killed 'em."

I said, "I know one thing. It's not gon kill me now, because I already quit it."

He said, "Yeah, well, it sure seems funny to me, you quittin' your job, talkin' about you can't do that and go to school. You ought to stop goin' to school. You didn't want to go to school when I was sendin' you there. Your Mama would take you in one door and you'd sneak out the other door. Even the truant officer couldn't keep you in school. Boy, I think you're dreamin'. You better stop all that dreamin' and go out there and get yourself a good job and keep it while you got it."

I knew that I couldn't talk to him and tell him what was really on my mind without going to battle with him, so I just said, "Yeah, Dad," to end it right there.

I remember when Pimp was thirteen or fourteen. He was in the eighth grade. He came home one day and said, "Mama, I think I'm gonna become an Air Force pilot and fly a jet plane."

It seemed a normal thing that any little boy might say to his mother and get some kind of encouragement, but that didn't happen in Pimp's case.

Mama told him, "Boy, don't you go wantin' things that ain't for you. You just go out there and get you a good job." A good job to Mama was a job making fifty or sixty dollars a week, and that was as much as anybody should have wanted, in Mama's opinion. Sixty dollars was damn good money. That was enough to retire off, the way they used to talk about it.

I guess I could understand their feeling this way. Their lives were lived according to the superstitions and fears that they had been taught when they were children coming up in the Carolina cotton fields. It was all right for them down there, in that time, in that place, but it wasn't worth a damn up in New York. I could understand why Mama couldn't understand Pimp and his troubles, because Mama had only gone through the fifth grade. Dad had only gone through the fourth grade. How could they understand Pimp when they couldn't even read his textbooks?

Mama and Dad and the people who had come to New York from the South about the time they did seemed to think it was wrong to want anything more out of life than some liquor on Saturday night. This was the stuff they did in the South. This was the sort of life they had lived on the plantations. They were trying to bring the down-home life up to Harlem. They had done it. But it just wasn't working. They couldn't understand it, and they weren't about to understand it. Liquor, religion, sex, and violence—this was all that life had been about to them. And a prayer that the right number would come out, that somebody would hit the sweepstakes or get lucky.

It seemed as though if I had stayed in Harlem all my life, I might have never known that there was anything else to life other than sex, religion, liquor, and violence. Sometimes I would try to tell Mama things in the slang terms. They had their own down-home slang expressions. I couldn't understand theirs too much, and they couldn't understand ours. The slang had changed. In this day when somebody would say something about a bad cat, they meant that he was good. Somebody would say, "That was some bad pot," meaning it was good. You really got high. Or somebody would go to the movie and see Sidney Poitier in a film,

and they'd say, "Man, that's a bad-doin' nigger." They didn't mean that he was running out in the street cutting somebody's throat, carrying a gun, and cursing. But this was all that a bad nigger meant to Mama and Dad and the people their age. It was the bad-nigger concept from the South, but it didn't mean that any more.

I couldn't get it over to Mama that things were changing. The bad nigger to my generation was a cat like Paul Robeson. To Mama, that was a nigger who was crazy, who would go out and marry some white woman. Mama and Dad would associate a nigger like this with the ones they saw hanging from a pine tree down in the Carolina woods with blood on his pants. They'd say this wasn't a bad nigger to them, this was a crazy nigger, one that was going to get himself hanged.

I could sense the fear in Mama's voice when I told her once that I wanted to be a psychologist.

She said, "Boy, you better stop that dreamin' and get all those crazy notions outta your head." She was scared. She had the idea that colored people weren't supposed to want anything like that. You were supposed to just want to work in fields or be happy to be a janitor.

I remember something she told Pimp. I think she thought she was giving Pimp something that he needed, and she felt big about it. "Now if you just get a job as a janitor, I'll be happy and satisfied," she said.

I jumped up when she said this, and I said, "Doesn't it matter whether he's satisfied or how he feels about it?"

Mama and Dad looked at me as if in two minutes time I'd be ready for Bellevue, or maybe they'd better call right away. They'd always look at me and say, "You better stop talkin' all that foolishness, boy. What's wrong with you? You better get all that stuff out of your head."

I remember the times I tried to explain these things to Mama, just what was happening in Harlem, just what was happening between my generation and hers. I would tell her, "Look, Mama, don't you remember when I use to play hookey from school, steal things, and stay out all night? Do you know why I was doin' that?"

She would look at me and ask, "Yeah, why?" sarcastically, as if I couldn't possibly tell her anything. I didn't understand anything that she couldn't understand.

I'd tell her about rebellion, and she'd say, "Look, don't be tellin' me about no rebellions and all that kind of business. You might know some big words, but you don't know what you're talkin' about. I know a whole lot of people go around using them old big words, and they don't know a damn thing what it's all about."

I'd say, "Look, Mama, when people start ruling people and they rule 'em wrong, in a way that's harmful to them, they have to stop them. They've got to rebel; they've got to get out from under their rule. Sometimes it requires a fight, but it's always going to require a little bit of commotion, a little bit of anger, and sometimes violence.

"You've got to stop them before they destroy you. That's all that's going on around here. Everybody is rebelling. You see all the young boys going around here using drugs. They're rebelling, that's all it is. They're rebelling against their parents. If there were any drugs around here when I was a little boy, I would've been using 'em too. I had to rebel. I had to get away from all that old down-home nonsense you been talking."

She'd say, "Boy, you don't know anything about that, and you ain't got no business calling it nonsense."

"Yeah, uh-huh. That's okay, Mama. Look, I'm trying to explain to you how this is. You gon listen?"

"I am listening, but I ain't hearing nothin' but a whole lot of foolishness."

I'd say something like, "Mama, you know and I know, these parents are talking about being good and doing right, but they're not being good."

"You must know more about what's goin' on around here than I do, 'cause I don't know no such thing."

"Look, Mama, don't you realize that whenever anybody starts talkin' some nonsense about 'be good, be good' and you can see that they're not bein' good, you're not gon pay too much attention to it? Right?"

She knew I was right, but she just didn't want to hear it. She'd say something like, "Boy, what you talkin' about?"

And I'd have to shout and say, "I'm talking about how you gon tell kids to be good when the kids are too hip not to see that the

parents aren't being so good their damn selves!"

She'd say, "Now, you wait a minute here, nigger. Don't you be gettin' so smart with me!" This was the way the discussion always went.

After I stopped and looked real disgusted, Mama would be ready to listen then. She would try to smooth my ruffled feathers. She'd say, "You mean to tell me that the only reason these kids is going around here messin' up, killin' themselves, and causin' their families a whole lotta trouble is that everybody's preachin' one thing and doin' another?"

I'd say, "It's something like that, but not all. Listen, what you mean is they're causin' their parents a lot of trouble. This is the way that most parents look at it. I don't think any parents look at the situation as if they could be causin' the kids some trouble and causin' them some embarrassment because they're going out doing the things that they're not suppose to do. But this is just what's happenin'."

Mama would say, "Ain't no kids got no business judgin' their parents."

"Mama, a lot of 'em aren't judgin' 'em. They're just going out and doing what they want to do too. They're not judgin' them; they're just gettin' revenge."

"Well, they ain't got no business tryin' to get revenge, because parents are grown, and they ain't got to answer to nobody's children." Then Mama would get all wound up, and she wouldn't listen to anything.

FOR DISCUSSION

1. Compare the values of the young Claude Brown with those of his parents. What are the causes of the different values?
2. What is the "race problem" that causes dissension between Claude Brown and his father?

Black
Experience

Bob Teague

(*1929–*   )

Bob Teague, a popular newscaster for NBC-TV in New York City, grew up in Milwaukee, Wisconsin, and graduated from the University of Wisconsin where he majored in journalism and played on the football team. His first newspaper job was with the *Milwaukee Journal;* later he became a reporter for *The New York Times.*

Teague lives with his wife, who dances for the Martha Graham Dance Company, and his son, Adam, to whom his book *Letters to a Black Boy* is addressed. He explains his purpose in writing these letters in the opening paragraph of the book: "What I hope to do is alert you. My theory is that if you can pick up some idea of what reality is like early, before it intrudes unannounced, you may not be caught off guard — unprepared and undone — as often as most men are."

FROM

Letters to a Black Boy

Dear Adam,

My prediction of wider horizons for black folk in your time perhaps sounded more optimistic than I intended. Not that my prediction went too far. But it should have been tempered with an important qualification:

Black participation in all areas of this society — jobs, housing, education and politics — will increase much faster than the acceptance of change by either race. Even when the day of full participation becomes possible — when all the roadblocks have been removed — black folk will need time to adjust. They will have to overcome their basic distrust and hostility toward whites, to learn to believe that the new America is not a big lie like the old one. Right now, those suspicions are born in our bones. Black men of the twenty-first century will need two or three generations to learn to believe that the newly opened doors are not a refinement of Mister Charlie's favorite prank: declaring a door open and then slamming it in any black face that does not belong to a superman.

Only when that legacy of distrust has been forgotten by a distant *second* generation of blacks to enjoy full participation all their lives,

59

will black folk truly be free. Only then will they begin behaving like the models of middle-class decency that Mister Charlie demands they be now while treating most blacks like animals.

Some distant generation of Mister Charlie's descendants will also have to overcome old habits that seem rooted in white souls: responding to myths about black folk instead of responding to the individual black person they happen to be facing.

All of this is to say, my son, that even if you were to become Vice President in the twenty-first century, you would probably still have to cope with a ridiculous amount of frustration and rejection that had nothing to do with you as a man.

Only last night, your daddy received another reminder that regardless of what laws are passed in Washington, D.C., to expand my acceptance in this society — and regardless of my credentials as a black man who has matched Mister Charlie in every game — real democracy depends on what happens day by day between individual members of different races.

I had just left the studio after my late newscast. I needed a taxi to get home to our apartment in Lower Manhattan.

At the corner of Broadway and 49th Street, I hailed an empty Yellow Cab as it approached from 50th Street, going downtown. The white man at the wheel seemed not to hear or see me. He passed me by.

I told myself, as I often do in these situations, that I should not jump to the conclusion that I was bypassed because I am black. After all, everyone in New York City gets passed up by a taxicab from time to time. It was possible that the man hadn't seen me.

Within two minutes, however, as three more empty Yellow Cabs turned me down, I was swearing under my breath. The punks won't let you live! Each of those three white drivers had seen me. I knew it. As they approached from 50th Street, each swerved his cab briefly in my direction at the curb; then, upon seeing that I was black, each turned his wheels the other way, looked straight ahead, pretended to be deaf and tromped down hard on the accelerator.

But the fourth cab in that hate parade had to stop about twenty yards past me, just across the 49th Street intersection, because of a red light. The traffic on Broadway was backed up from the light at 48th Street, a block ahead. I walked across the intersection

and reached for the door handle on the cab. The driver turned
and tried to push down the button that would lock it. But I was
faster on the draw. As I climbed into the back seat, he shouted
a barrage of insults and curses.

"And besides," he ended, "I'm going off duty right now!"

I refused to budge. "Then why in the hell didn't you flash your
damn off-duty sign?" I yelled. Then I slammed the door behind
me. "If you don't take me where I want to go," I threatened, reading
his name and number on the license affixed to the dashboard, "I'll
turn you in at the Hack Bureau. You know damn well what you
did is against the law."

The driver — let's call him Fred — was stopped in mid-sentence
by the sound of my voice. Not by what I said.

"Oh, it's *you*," he said sheepishly. "I didn't recognize you at
first until I heard your voice. I'd know that voice anywhere. On
the moon even. You really do a great job with the news. I watch
you every night when I'm not out hacking so late like tonight
and. . . ."

I said nothing. Fred kept chattering. I was more than a little
uncertain about how to take it.

The light turned green at 48th Street. Traffic on Broadway began
moving, and Fred moved with it. Still talking, still mixing flatteries
with apologies.

"Gee, I'd give anything if I hadn't made that mistake," he went
on. "I'm really and truly sorry. And you know what makes it
so funny is that I've had you in my cab before. I picked you
up just outside the studio one night maybe five, six months ago.
You're going to the edge of Chinatown, right? I took you there
that time. And like I told you then, me and my wife we watch
you all the time. Man, wait'll I tell her I had you in my cab again.
She's always saying how what a handsome guy you are on TV.
Sexy and all that, she says. And she gave me a bad time for not
getting your autograph the last time I took you home. This ride
is on me, by the way. I couldn't think of taking any money after
what happened. It's a real pleasure and thrill just having you in
my cab. And. . . ."

I didn't feel flattered. I felt angry, indignant and embarrassed.
Gradually, however, Fred's nonstop apology did confuse the situation. Should I be a nice guy and accept his apology? Should I

spit in his face? Should I chew him out? Should I give him a calm little lecture on how being treated like that was the stuff that drove black men to madness — the stuff that riots are made of? Or should I say nothing at all and simply take my case to the Hack Bureau?

Finally, perhaps two miles from where we had met, Fred paused to breathe and light a smoke. He passed the pack over his shoulder. I took one and lit up, too.

"Gee, I really wish that hadn't happened back there," he said again.

"It's all right, Fred," I said. "Let's forget it. But remember it the next time you see a black man standing on a corner. And try to imagine how you'd feel if something like that happened to you almost every time you left your house."

Fred apologized again. And again. And again.

"It's all right," I said. "Let's forget it."

When we got to the corner near my apartment, the meter read $1.85. Fred wouldn't accept my money.

"Oh, no," he said. "This is on me. A real pleasure having you in my cab."

I hesitated, still uncertain. He sounded as if he were truly repentant. But was he really? And if so, did it matter? Could he have been thinking that he had tried to pass up a black man who was too well known to be called a liar if the case ever went before the Hack Bureau?

"I can't take your money," Fred went on. "But I would appreciate an autograph for my missus, if you don't mind."

Here it was. The right moment and exactly the right place to spit in his face. But I couldn't do it. Let your triumph, I told myself, be the knowledge that no matter what they do, they can't turn you into something just as ugly.

I signed the pad he offered. "Here you are," I said as evenly as possible for me. "And good night."

Fred thanked me and made one final apology before driving off.

As I started walking toward the entrance of our apartment building, I had a curious sense of having lost something of myself. And I knew that I would never get it back.

FOR DISCUSSION

1. What does Teague mean in the last paragraph by his "curious sense of having lost something of myself"? What has he lost? Would he have lost it if he had acted differently toward the cab driver?
2. Teague says that black participation in American society "will increase much faster than the acceptance of change by either race." What precisely does he mean? Do you agree?

Richard Wright
(1908–1960)

A self-declared "rootless man," Richard Wright felt alienated from American and from African cultures. Born on a farm in Mississippi, Wright had an unstable childhood; he lived part of his youth in an orphanage until he was sent to live with his grandmother. He later worked at a succession of jobs and suffered humiliation from several white employers. Hoping that "life could be lived with dignity," Wright moved to Chicago in 1927, adopted Marxist ideas, and began to publish poems and essays in radical magazines such as *Left Front* and *New Masses,* and in the *Daily Worker.* During the thirties, he rejected his affiliation with the Communist Party. He became director of the Federal Negro Theater and joined the Federal Writers Project. In 1938, he published *Uncle Tom's Children,* a collection of stories about sharecroppers in the rural South. *Native Son,* which followed in 1940, dealt with the economic plight of urban blacks. Wright's rejection of middle class values was further developed in his novel, *The Outsider.* In voluntary exile from what he considered American racism, Wright spent the last decade of his life in France and England. During that period he produced the novels *The Long Dream* and *Lawd Today;* a collection of stories, *Eight Men* (from which the following selection was taken); and the sociological studies *Black Power* and *White Man, Listen!* The first major author to deal with the economic frustration of ghetto blacks, Wright has been a significant influence on black writers who have followed him.

The Man Who Went
to Chicago

Christmas came and I was once more called to the post office for temporary work. This time I met many young white men and we discussed world happenings, the vast armies of unemployed, the rising tide of radical action. I now detected a change in the attitudes of the whites I met; their privations were making them regard Negroes with new eyes, and, for the first time, I was invited to their homes.

When the work in the post office ended, I was assigned by the relief system as an orderly to a medical research institute in one of the largest and wealthiest hospitals in Chicago. I cleaned operating rooms, dog, rat, mice, cat, and rabbit pans, and fed guinea pigs. Four of us Negroes worked there and we occupied an underworld position, remembering that we must restrict ourselves — when not engaged upon some task — to the basement corridors, so that we would not mingle with white nurses, doctors, or visitors.

The sharp line of racial division drawn by the hospital authorities came to me the first morning when I walked along an underground corridor and saw two long lines of women coming toward me. A line of white girls marched past, clad in starched uniforms that gleamed white; their faces were alert, their step quick, their bodies lean and shapely, their shoulders erect, their faces lit with the light of purpose. And after them came a line of black girls, old, fat, dressed in ragged gingham, walking loosely, carrying tin cans of soap powder, rags, mops, brooms . . . . I wondered what law of the universe kept them from being mixed? The sun would not have stopped shining had there been a few black girls in the first line, and the earth would not have stopped whirling on its axis had there been a few white girls in the second line. But the two lines I saw graded social status in purely racial terms.

Of the three Negroes who worked with me, one was a boy about my own age, Bill, who was either sleepy or drunk most of the time. Bill straightened his hair and I suspected that he kept a bottle hidden somewhere in the piles of hay which we fed to the guinea pigs. He did not like me and I did not like him, though I tried harder than he to conceal my dislike. We had nothing in common except that we were both black and lost. While I contained my frustration, he drank to drown his. Often I tried to talk to him, tried in simple words to convey to him some of my ideas, and he would listen in sullen silence. Then one day he came to me with an angry look on his face.

"I got it," he said.

"You've got what?" I asked.

"This old race problem you keep talking about," he said.

"What about it?"

"Well, it's this way," he explained seriously. "Let the government give every man a gun and five bullets, then let us all start over again. Make it just like it was in the beginning. The ones who come out on top, white or black, let them rule."

His simplicity terrified me. I had never met a Negro who was so irredeemably brutalized. I stopped pumping my ideas into Bill's brain for fear that the fumes of alcohol might send him reeling toward some fantastic fate.

The two other Negroes were elderly and had been employed in the institute for fifteen years or more. One was Brand, a short, black, morose bachelor; the other was Cooke, a tall, yellow, spectacled fellow who spent his spare time keeping track of world events through the Chicago *Tribune*. Brand and Cooke hated each other for a reason that I was never able to determine, and they spent a good part of each day quarreling.

When I began working at the institute, I recalled my adolescent dream of wanting to be a medical research worker. Daily I saw young Jewish boys and girls receiving instruction in chemistry and medicine that the average black boy or girl could never receive. When I was alone, I wandered and poked my fingers into strange chemicals, watched intricate machines trace red and black lines on ruled paper. At times I paused and stared at the walls of the rooms, at the floors, at the wide desks at which the white doctors sat; and I realized — with a feeling that I could never quite get used to — that I was looking at the world of another race.

My interest in what was happening in the institute amused the three other Negroes with whom I worked. They had no curiosity about "white folks' things," while I wanted to know if the dogs being treated for diabetes were getting well; if the rats and mice in which cancer had been induced showed any signs of responding to treatment. I wanted to know the principle that lay behind the Ascheim-Zondek tests that were made with rabbits, the Wassermann tests that were made with guinea pigs. But when I asked a timid question I found that even Jewish doctors had learned to imitate the sadistic method of humbling a Negro that the others had cultivated.

"If you know too much, boy, your brains might explode," a doctor said one day.

Each Saturday morning I assisted a young Jewish doctor in slitting the vocal cords of a fresh batch of dogs from the city pound. The object was to devocalize the dogs so that their howls would not disturb the patients in the other parts of the hospital. I held each dog as the doctor injected Nembutal into its veins to make it unconscious; then I held the dog's jaws open as the doctor inserted the scalpel and severed the vocal cords. Later, when the dogs came to, they would lift their heads to the ceiling and gape in a soundless wail. The sight became lodged in my imagination as a symbol of silent suffering.

To me Nembutal was a powerful and mysterious liquid, but when I asked questions about its properties I could not obtain a single intelligent answer. The doctor simply ignored me with:

"Come on. Bring me the next dog. I haven't got all day."

One Saturday morning, after I had held the dogs for their vocal cords to be slit, the doctor left the Nembutal on a bench. I picked it up, uncorked it, and smelled it. It was odorless. Suddenly Brand ran to me with a stricken face.

"What're you doing?" he asked.

"I was smelling this stuff to see if it had any odor," I said.

"Did you really smell it?" he asked me.

"Yes."

"Oh, God!" he exclaimed.

"What's the matter?" I asked.

"You shouldn't've done that!" he shouted.

"Why?"

He grabbed my arm and jerked me across the room.

"Come on!" he yelled, snatching open the door.

"What's the matter?" I asked.

"I gotta get you to a doctor 'fore it's too late," he gasped.

Had my foolish curiosity made me inhale something dangerous?

"But — is it poisonous?"

"Run, boy!" he said, pulling me. "You'll fall dead."

Filled with fear, with Brand pulling my arm, I rushed out of the room, raced across a rear areaway, into another room, then down a long corridor. I wanted to ask Brand what symptoms I must expect, but we were running too fast. Brand finally stopped, gasping for breath. My heart beat wildly and my blood pounded in my head. Brand then dropped to the concrete floor, stretched out on his back, and yelled with laughter, shaking all over. He beat his fists against the concrete; he moaned, giggled; he kicked.

I tried to master my outrage, wondering if some of the white doctors had told him to play the joke. He rose and wiped tears from his eyes, still laughing. I walked away from him. He knew that I was angry and he followed me.

"Don't get mad," he gasped through his laughter.

"Go to hell," I said.

"I couldn't help it," he giggled. "You looked at me like you'd believe anything I said. Man, you was scared."

He leaned against the wall, laughing again, stomping his feet. I was angry, for I felt that he would spread the story. I knew that Bill and Cooke never ventured beyond the safe bounds of Negro living, and they would never blunder into anything like this. And if they heard about this, they would laugh for months.

"Brand, if you mention this, I'll kill you," I swore.

"You ain't mad?" he asked, laughing, staring at me through tears.

Sniffing, Brand walked ahead of me. I followed him back into the room that housed the dogs. All day, while at some task, he would pause and giggle, then smother the giggling with his hand, looking at me out of the corner of his eyes, shaking his head. He laughed at me for a week. I kept my temper and let him amuse himself. I finally found out the properties of Nembutal by consulting medical books; but I never told Brand.

One summer morning, just as I began work, a young Jewish boy came to me with a stop watch in his hand.

"Dr. _____ wants me to time you when you clean a room," he said. "We're trying to make the institute more efficient."

"I'm doing my work and getting through on time," I said.

"This is the boss's order," he said.

"Why don't you work for a change?" I blurted, angry.

"Now, look," he said. "*This* is my work. Now *you* work."

I got a mop and pail, sprayed a room with disinfectant, and scrubbed at coagulated blood and hardened dog, rat, and rabbit feces. The normal temperature of a room was ninety, but, as the sun beat down upon the skylights, the temperature rose above a hundred. Stripped to my waist, I slung the mop, moving steadily like a machine, hearing the boy press the button on the stop watch as I finished cleaning a room.

"Well, how is it?" I asked.

"It took you seventeen minutes to clean that last room," he said. "That ought to be the time for each room."

"But that room was not very dirty," I said.

"You have seventeen rooms to clean," he went on as though I had not spoken. "Seventeen times seventeen make four hours and forty-nine minutes." He wrote upon a little pad. "After lunch, clean the five flights of stone stairs. I timed a boy who scrubbed one step and multiplied that time by the number of steps. You ought to be through by six."

"Suppose I want relief?" I asked.

"You'll manage," he said and left.

Never had I felt so much the slave as when I scoured those stone steps each afternoon. Working against time, I would wet five steps, sprinkle soap powder, and then a white doctor or nurse would come along and, instead of avoiding the soapy steps, would walk on them and track the dirty water onto the steps that I had already cleaned. To obviate this, I cleaned but two steps at a time, a distance over which a ten-year-old child could step. But it did no good. The white people still plopped their feet down into the dirty water and muddied the other clean steps. If I ever really hotly hated unthinking whites, it was then. Not once during my entire stay at the institute did a single white person show enough courtesy to avoid a wet step. I would be on my knees, scrubbing, sweating, pouring out what limited energy my body could wring from my meager diet, and I would hear feet approaching. I would pause and curse with tense lips.

Sometimes a sadistically observant white man would notice that he had tracked dirty water up the steps, and he would look back down at me and smile and say:

"Boy, we sure keep you busy, don't we?"

And I would not be able to answer.

The feud that went on between Brand and Cooke continued. Although they were working daily in a building where scientific history was being made, the light of curiosity was never in their eyes. They were conditioned to their racial "place," had learned to see only a part of the whites and the white world; and the whites, too, had learned to see only a part of the lives of the blacks and their world.

Perhaps Brand and Cooke, lacking interests that could absorb them, fuming like children over trifles, simply invented their hate of each other in order to have something to feel deeply about. Or perhaps there was in them a vague tension stemming from their chronically frustrating way of life, a pain whose cause they did not know; and, like those devocalized dogs, they would whirl and snap at the air when their old pain struck them. Anyway, they argued about the weather, sports, sex, war, race, politics, and religion; neither of them knew much about the subjects they debated, but it seemed that the less they knew the better they could argue.

The tug of war between the two elderly men reached a climax one winter day at noon. It was incredibly cold and an icy gale swept up and down the Chicago streets with blizzard force. The door of the animal-filled room was locked, for we always insisted that we be allowed one hour in which to eat and rest. Bill and I were sitting on wooden boxes, eating our lunches out of paper bags. Brand was washing his hands at the sink. Cooke was sitting on a rickety stool, munching an apple and reading the Chicago *Tribune.*

Now and then a devocalized dog lifted his nose to the ceiling and howled soundlessly. The room was filled with many rows of high steel tiers. Perched upon each of these tiers were layers of steel cages containing the dogs, rats, mice, rabbits, and guinea pigs. Each cage was labeled in some indecipherable scientific jargon. Along the walls of the room were long charts with zigzagging red and black lines that traced the success or failure of some experiment. The lonely piping of guinea pigs floated unheeded about us. Hay rustled as a rabbit leaped restlessly about in its pen. A rat scampered around in its steel prison. Cooke tapped the newspaper for attention.

"It says here," Cooke mumbled through a mouthful of apple, "that this is the coldest day since 1888."

Bill and I sat unconcerned. Brand chuckled softly.

"What in hell you laughing about?" Cooke demanded of Brand.

"You can't believe what that damn *Tribune* says," Brand said.

"How come I can't?" Cooke demanded. "It's the world's greatest newspaper."

Brand did not reply; he shook his head pityingly and chuckled again.

"Stop that damn laughing at me!" Cooke said angrily.

"I laugh as much as I wanna," Brand said. "You don't know what you talking about. The *Herald-Examiner* says it's the coldest day since 1873."

"But the *Trib* oughta know," Cooke countered. "It's older'n that *Examiner.*"

"That damn *Trib* don't know nothing!" Brand drowned out Cooke's voice.

"How in hell you know?" Cooke asked with rising anger.

The argument waxed until Cooke shouted that if Brand did not shut up he was going to "cut his black throat."

Brand whirled from the sink, his hands dripping soapy water, his eyes blazing.

"Take that back," Brand said.

"I take nothing back! What you wanna do about it?" Cooke taunted.

The two elderly Negroes glared at each other. I wondered if the quarrel was really serious, or if it would turn out harmlessly as so many others had done.

Suddenly Cooke dropped the Chicago *Tribune* and pulled a long knife from his pocket; his thumb pressed a button and a gleaming steel blade leaped out. Brand stepped back quickly and seized an ice pick that was stuck in a wooden board above the sink.

"Put that knife down," Brand said.

"Stay 'way from me, or I'll cut your throat," Cooke warned.

Brand lunged with the ice pick. Cooke dodged out of range. They circled each other like fighters in a prize ring. The cancerous and tubercular rats and mice leaped about in their cages. The guinea pigs whistled in fright. The diabetic dogs bared their teeth and barked soundlessly in our direction. The Aschheim-Zondek rabbits flopped their ears and tried to hide in the corners of their pens. Cooke now crouched and sprang forward wih the knife. Bill and I jumped to our feet, speechless with surprise. Brand retreated. The eyes of both men were hard and unblinking; they were breathing deeply.

"Say, cut it out!" I called in alarm.

"Them damn fools is really fighting," Bill said in amazement.

Slashing at each other, Brand and Cooke surged up and down the aisles of steel tiers. Suddenly Brand uttered a bellow and charged into Cooke and swept him violently backward. Cooke grasped Brand's hand to keep the ice pick from sinking into his chest. Brand broke free and charged Cooke again, sweeping him into an animal-filled steel tier. The tier balanced itself on its edge for an indecisive moment, then toppled.

Like kingpins, one steel tier lammed into another, then they all crashed to the floor with a sound as of the roof falling. The whole aspect of the room altered quicker than the eye could follow. Brand and Cooke stood stock-still, their eyes fastened upon each other, their pointed weapons raised; but they were dimly aware of the havoc that churned about them.

The steel tiers lay jumbled; the doors of the cages swung open. Rats and mice and dogs and rabbits moved over the floor in wild panic. The Wassermann guinea pigs were squealing as though judgment day had come. Here and there an animal had been crushed beneath a cage.

All four of us looked at one another. We knew what this meant. We might lose our jobs. We were already regarded as black dunces; and if the doctors saw this mess they would take it as final proof. Bill rushed to the door to make sure that it was locked. I glanced at the clock and saw that it was 12:30. We had one half hour of grace.

"Come on," Bill said uneasily. "We got to get this place cleaned."

Brand and Cooke stared at each other, both doubting.

"Give me your knife, Cooke," I said.

"Naw! Take Brand's ice pick *first*," Cooke said.

"The hell you say!" Brand said. "Take his knife *first!*"

A knock sounded at the door.

"Sssssh," Bill said.

We waited. We heard footsteps going away. We'll all lose our jobs, I thought.

Persuading the fighters to surrender their weapons was a difficult task, but at last it was done and we could begin to set things right. Slowly Brand stooped and tugged at one end of a steel tier. Cooke stooped to help him. Both men seemed to be acting in a dream. Soon, however, all four of us were working frantically, watching the clock.

As we labored we conspired to keep the fight a secret; we agreed to tell the doctors — if any should ask — that we had not been in the room during our lunch hour; we felt that that lie would explain why no one had unlocked the door when the knock had come.

We righted the tiers and replaced the cages; then we were faced with the impossible task of sorting the cancerous rats and mice, the diabetic dogs, the Aschheim-Zondek rabbits, and the Wassermann guinea pigs. Whether we kept our jobs or not depended upon how shrewdly we could cover up all evidence of the fight. It was pure guesswork, but we had to try to put the animals back into the correct cages. We knew that certain rats or mice went into certain cages, but we did not know *what* rat or mouse went into *what* cage. We did not know a tubercular mouse from a cancerous mouse — the white doctors had made sure that we would not know. They had never taken time to answer a single question; though we worked in the institute, we were as remote from the meaning of the experiments as if we lived in the moon. The doctors had laughed at what they felt was our childlike interest in the fate of the animals.

First we sorted the dogs; that was fairly easy, for we could remember the size and color of most of them. But the rats and mice and guinea pigs baffled us completely.

We put our heads together and pondered, down in the underworld of the great scientific institute. It was a strange scientific conference; the fate of the entire medical research institute rested in our ignorant, black hands.

We remembered the number of rats, mice, or guinea pigs — we had to handle them several times a day — that went into a given cage, and we supplied the number helter-skelter from those animals that we could catch running loose on the floor. We discovered that many rats, mice, and guinea pigs were missing — they had been killed in the scuffle. We solved that problem by taking healthy stock from other cages and putting them into cages with sick animals. We repeated this process until we were certain that, numerically at least, all the animals with which the doctors were experimenting were accounted for.

The rabbits came last. We broke the rabbits down into two general groups; those that had fur on their bellies and those that did not. We knew that all those rabbits that had shaven bellies — our scientific knowledge adequately covered this point because it was our job to shave the rabbits — were undergoing the Aschheim-Zondek tests. But in what pen did a given rabbit belong? We did not know. I solved the problem very simply. I counted the shaven rabbits; they numbered seventeen. I counted the pens labeled "Aschheim-Zondek," then proceeded to drop a shaven rabbit into each pen at random. And again we were numerically successful. At least white America had taught us how to count. . . .

Lastly we carefully wrapped all the dead animals in newspapers and hid their bodies in a garbage can.

At a few minutes to one the room was in order; that is, the kind of order that we four Negroes could figure out. I unlocked the door and we sat waiting, whispering, vowing secrecy, wondering what the reaction of the doctors would be.

Finally a doctor came, gray-haired, white-coated, spectacled, efficient, serious, taciturn, bearing a tray upon which sat a bottle of mysterious fluid and a hypodermic needle.

"My rats, please."

Cooke shuffled forward to serve him. We held our breath. Cooke got the cage which he knew the doctor always called for at that hour and brought it forward. One by one, Cooke took out the rats and held them as the doctor solemnly injected the mysterious fluid under their skins.

"Thank you, Cooke," the doctor murmured.

"Not at all, sir," Cooke mumbled with a suppressed gasp.

When the doctor had gone we looked at one another, hardly daring to believe that our secret would be kept. We were so anxious that we did not know whether to curse or laugh. Another doctor came.

"Give me A-Z rabbit number 14."

"Yes, sir," I said.

I brought him the rabbit and he took it upstairs to the operating room. We waited for repercussions. None came.

All that afternoon the doctors came and went. I would run into the room — stealing a few seconds from my step-scrubbing — and ask what progress was being made and would learn that the doctors had detected nothing. At quitting time we felt triumphant.

"They won't ever know," Cooke boasted in a whisper.

I saw Brand stiffen. I knew that he was aching to dispute Cooke's optimism, but the memory of the fight he had just had was so fresh in his mind that he could not speak.

Another day went by and nothing happened. Then another day. The doctors examined the animals and wrote in their little black books, in their big black books, and continued to trace red and black lines upon the charts.

A week passed and we felt out of danger. Not one question had been asked.

Of course, we four black men were much too modest to make our contribution known, but we often wondered what went on in the laboratories after that secret disaster. Was some scientific hypothesis, well on its way to validation and ultimate public use, discarded because of unexpected findings on that cold winter day? Was some tested principle given a new and strange refinement because of fresh, remarkable evidence? Did some brooding research worker — those who held stop watches and slopped their feet carelessly in the water of the steps I tried so hard to keep clean — get a wild, if brief, glimpse of a new scientific truth? Well, we never heard . . . .

I brooded upon whether I should have gone to the director's office and told him what had happened, but each time I thought of it I remembered that the director had been the man who had ordered the boy to stand over me while I was working and time my movements with a stop watch. He did not regard me as a human being. I did not share his world. I earned thirteen dollars a week and I had to support four people with it, and should I risk that thirteen dollars by acting idealistically? Brand and Cooke would have hated me and would have eventually driven me from the job had I "told" on them. The hospital kept us four Negroes as though we were close kin to the animals we tended, huddled together down in the underworld corridors of the hospital, separated by a vast psychological distance from the significant processes of the rest of the hospital — just as America had kept us locked in the dark underworld of American life for three hundred years — and we had made our own code of ethics, values, loyalty.

FOR DISCUSSION

1. In this selection, Wright describes a hospital divided into two "worlds": the basement "underworld" and the "world" of the building above. What is life like in each of these worlds? What do the two worlds symbolize?
2. What effect does the "underworld" have on the people who live in it? Does it have similar effects on each of the characters?
3. After the fight, the black men return the animals to the wrong cages, and the white researchers never know the difference. What is Wright satirizing in this episode?

James Baldwin

(*1924–*   )

One of America's foremost novelists and essayists, James Baldwin first began writing in high school, where he was editor of his school magazine. After graduation, he worked as an office boy, a factory worker, a dishwasher, and a waiter while he wrote in his spare time. In 1948, Baldwin won a Eugene Saxton Fellowship and moved to Europe to begin a full-time writing career; he remained in Europe until 1956. During this period, Baldwin published his first novel, *Go Tell It On the Mountain,* and his first book of essays, *Notes of a Native Son.* His next two books of essays, *Nobody Knows My Name* and *The Fire Next Time,* established his reputation as a writer and brought him recognition as an articulate spokesman for black protest. The author of two plays, *Amen Corner* and *Blues for Mr. Charlie,* and novels which include *Tell Me How Long the Train's Been Gone,* Baldwin portrays the black man's search for identity in America. Baldwin repeatedly insists that the real victim of bigotry is the white man who hides his weaknesses under his myth of superiority. Active in civil rights, Baldwin has lectured for the Congress of Racial Equality, supported the 1963 march on Washington, and served as a member of the national advisory board of CORE. He has also been a member of the National Committee for a Sane Nuclear Policy.

Notes of a Native Son

On the 29th of July, in 1943, my father died. On the same day, a few hours later, his last child was born. Over a month before this, while all our energies were concentrated in waiting for these events, there had been, in Detroit, one of the bloodiest race riots of the century. A few hours after my father's funeral, while he lay in state in the undertaker's chapel, a race riot broke out in Harlem. On the morning of the 3rd of August, we drove my father to the graveyard through a wilderness of smashed plate glass.

The day of my father's funeral had also been my nineteenth birthday. As we drove him to the graveyard, the spoils of injustice, anarchy, discontent, and hatred were all around us. It seemed to me that God himself had devised, to mark my father's end, the most sustained and brutally dissonant of codas. And it seemed to me, too, that the violence which rose all about us as my father left the world had been devised as a corrective for the pride of his eldest son. I had declined to believe in that apocalypse which had been central to my father's vision; very well, life seemed to be saying, here is something that will certainly pass for an apocalypse until the real thing comes along. I had inclined to be contemptuous of my father for the conditions of his life, for the conditions of our lives. When his life had ended I began to wonder about that life and also, in a new way, to be apprehensive about my own.

I had not known my father very well. We had got on badly, partly because we shared, in our different fashions, the vice of stubborn pride. When he was dead I realized that I had hardly ever spoken to him. When he had been dead a long time I began to wish I had. It seems to be typical of life in America, where opportunities, real and fancied, are thicker than anywhere else on the globe, that the second generation has no time to talk to the first. No one, including my father, seems to have known exactly how old he was, but his mother had been born during slavery. He was of the first generation of free men. He, along with thousands of other Negroes, came North after 1919 and I was part of that generation which had never seen the landscape of what Negroes sometimes call the Old Country.

He had been born in New Orleans and had been a quite young man there during the time that Louis Armstrong, a boy, was running errands for the dives and honky-tonks of what was always presented to me as one of the most wicked of cities — to this day, whenever I think of New Orleans, I also helplessly think of Sodom and Gomorrah. My father never mentioned Louis Armstrong, except to forbid us to play his records; but there was a picture of him on our wall for a long time. One of my father's strong-willed female relatives had placed it there and forbade my father to take it down. He never did, but he eventually maneuvered her out of the house and when, some years later, she was in trouble and near death, he refused to do anything to help her.

He was, I think, very handsome. I gather this from photographs and from my own memories of him, dressed in his Sunday best and on his way to preach a sermon somewhere, when I was little. Handsome, proud, and ingrown, "like a toe-nail," somebody said. But he looked to me, as I grew older, like pictures I had seen of African tribal chieftains: he really should have been naked, with war-paint on and barbaric mementos, standing among spears. He could be chilling in the pulpit and indescribably cruel in his personal life, and he was certainly the most bitter man I have ever met; yet it must be said that there was something else in him, buried in him, which lent him his tremendous power and, even, a rather crushing charm. It had something to do with his blackness, I think — he was very black — with his blackness and his beauty, and with the fact that he knew that he was black but did not know that he was beautiful. He claimed to be proud of his blackness but it had also been the cause of much humiliation and it had fixed bleak boundaries to his life. He was not a young man when we were growing up and he had already suffered many kinds of ruin; in his outrageously demanding and protective way he loved his children, who were black like him and menaced, like him; and all these things sometimes showed in his face when he tried, never to my knowledge with any success, to establish contact with any of us. When he took one of his children on his knee to play, the child always became fretful and began to cry; when he tried to help one of us with our homework the absolutely unabating tension which emanated from him caused our minds and our tongues to become paralyzed, so that he, scarcely knowing why, flew into a rage and the child, not knowing why, was punished. If it ever entered his head to bring a surprise home for his children, it was, almost unfailingly, the wrong surprise and even the big watermelons he often brought home on his back in the summertime led to the most appalling scenes. I do not remember, in all those years, that one of his children was ever glad to see him come home. From what I was able to gather of his early life, it seemed that this inability to establish contact with other people had always marked him and had been one of the things which had driven him out of New Orleans. There was something in him, therefore, groping and tentative, which was never expressed and which was buried with him. One saw it most clearly when he was facing new people and hoping to impress them. But he never did, not for long. We went from church to smaller and more improbable church; he found himself in less and less demand as a minister, and by the time he died none of his friends had come to see him for a long time. He had lived and died in an intolerable bitterness of spirit and it frightened me, as we drove him to the graveyard through those unquiet, ruined streets, to see how powerful and overflowing this bitterness could be and to realize that this bitterness now was mine.

When he died I had been away from home for a little over a year. In that year I had had time to become aware of the meaning of all my father's bitter warnings, had discovered the secret of his proudly pursed lips and rigid carriage: I had discovered the weight of white people in the world. I saw that this had been

for my ancestors and now would be for me an awful thing to
live with and that the bitterness which had helped to kill my father
could also kill me.

He had been ill a long time — in the mind, as we now realized
reliving instances of his fantastic intransigence in the new light
of his affliction and endeavoring to feel a sorrow for him which
never, quite, came true. We had not known that he was being
eaten up by paranoia, and the discovery that his cruelty, to our
bodies and our minds, had been one of the symptoms of his illness
was not, then, enough to enable us to forgive him. The younger
children felt, quite simply, relief that he would not be coming home
anymore. My mother's observation that it was he, after all, who
had kept them alive all these years meant nothing because the
problems of keeping children alive are not real for children. The
older children felt, with my father gone, that they could invite
their friends to the house without fear that their friends would
be insulted or, as had sometimes happened with me, being told
that their friends were in league with the devil and intended to
rob our family of everything we owned. (I didn't fail to wonder,
and it made me hate him, what on earth we owned that anybody
else would want.)

His illness was beyond all hope of healing before anyone realized
that he was ill. He had always been so strange and had lived,
like a prophet, in such unimaginably close communion with the
Lord that his long silences which were punctuated by moans and
hallelujahs and snatches of old songs while he sat at the living-room
window never seemed odd to us. It was not until he refused to
eat because, he said, his family was trying to poison him that my
mother was forced to accept as a fact what had, until then, been
only an unwilling suspicion. When he was committed, it was
discovered that he had tuberculosis and, as it turned out, the disease
of his mind allowed the disease of his body to destroy him. For
the doctors could not force him to eat, either, and, though he was
fed intravenously, it was clear from the beginning that there was
no hope for him.

In my mind's eye I could see him, sitting at the window, locked
up in his terrors; hating and fearing every living soul including
his children who had betrayed him, too, by reaching towards the
world which had despised him. There were nine of us. I began

to wonder what it could have felt like for such a man to have had nine children whom he could barely feed. He used to make little jokes about our poverty, which never, of course, seemed very funny to us; they could not have seemed very funny to him, either, or else our too feeble response to them would never have caused such rages. He spent great energy and achieved, to our chagrin, no small amount of success in keeping us away from the people who surrounded us, people who had all-night rent parties to which we listened when we should have been sleeping, people who cursed and drank and flashed razor blades on Lenox Avenue. He could not understand why, if they had so much energy to spare, they could not use it to make their lives better. He treated almost everybody on our block with a most uncharitable asperity and neither they, nor, of course, their children were slow to reciprocate.

The only white people who came to our house were welfare workers and bill collectors. It was almost always my mother who dealt with them, for my father's temper, which was at the mercy of his pride, was never to be trusted. It was clear that he felt their very presence in his home to be a violation: this was conveyed by his carriage, almost ludicrously stiff, and by his voice, harsh and vindictively polite. When I was around nine or ten I wrote a play which was directed by a young, white schoolteacher, a woman, who then took an interest in me, and gave me books to read and, in order to corroborate my theatrical bent, decided to take me to see what she somewhat tactlessly referred to as "real" plays. Theater-going was forbidden in our house, but, with the really cruel intuitiveness of a child, I suspected that the color of this woman's skin would carry the day for me. When, at school, she suggested taking me to the theater, I did not, as I might have done if she had been a Negro, find a way of discouraging her, but agreed that she should pick me up at my house one evening. I then, very cleverly, left all the rest to my mother, who suggested to my father, as I knew she would, that it would not be very nice to let such a kind woman make the trip for nothing. Also, since it was a schoolteacher, I imagine that my mother countered the idea of sin with the idea of "education," which word, even with my father, carried a kind of bitter weight.

Before the teacher came my father took me aside to ask *why* she was coming, what *interest* she could possibly have in our house, in a boy like me. I said I didn't know but I, too, suggested that it had something to do with education. And I understood that my father was waiting for me to say something — I didn't quite know what; perhaps that I wanted his protection against this teacher and her "education." I said none of these things and the teacher came and we went out. It was clear, during the brief interview in our living room, that my father was agreeing very much against his will and that he would have refused permission if he had dared. The fact that he did not dare caused me to despise him: I had no way of knowing that he was facing in that living room a wholly unprecedented and frightening situation.

Later, when my father had been laid off from his job, this woman became very important to us. She was really a very sweet and generous woman and went to a great deal of trouble to be of help to us, particularly during one awful winter. My mother called her by the highest name she knew: she said she was a "Christian." My father could scarcely disagree but during the four or five years of our relatively close association he never trusted her and was always trying to surprise in her open, Midwestern face the genuine, cunningly hidden, and hideous motivation. In later years, particularly when it began to be clear that this "education" of mine was going to lead me to perdition, he became more explicit and warned me that my white friends in high school were not really my friends and that I would see, when I was older, how white people would do anything to keep a Negro down. Some of them could be nice, he admitted, but none of them were to be trusted and most of them were not even nice. The best thing was to have as little to do with them as possible. I did not feel this way and I was certain, in my innocence, that I never would.

But the year which preceded my father's death had made a great change in my life. I had been living in New Jersey, working in defense plants, working and living among Southerners, white and black. I knew about the South, of course, and about how Southerners treated Negroes and how they expected them to behave, but it had never entered my mind that anyone would look at me and expect *me* to behave that way. I learned in New Jersey that to be a Negro meant, precisely, that one was never looked at but was simply at the mercy of the reflexes the color of one's skin caused in other people. I acted in New Jersey as I had always acted, that is as though I thought a great deal of myself — I had to *act* that way — with results that were, simply, unbelievable. I had scarcely arrived before I had earned the enmity, which was extraordinarily ingenious, of all my superiors and nearly all my co-workers. In the beginning, to make matters worse, I simply did not know what was happening. I did not know what I had done, and I shortly began to wonder what *anyone* could possibly do, to bring about such unanimous, active, and unbearably vocal hostility. I knew about jim-crow but I had never experienced it. I went to the same self-service restaurant three times and stood with all the Princeton boys before the counter, waiting for a hamburger and coffee; it was always an extraordinarily long time before anything was set before me; but it was not until the fourth visit that I learned that, in fact, nothing had ever been set before me: I had simply picked something up. Negroes were not served there, I was told, and they had been waiting for me to realize that I was always the only Negro present. Once I was told this, I determined to go there all the time. But now they were ready for me and, though some dreadful scenes were subsequently enacted in that restaurant, I never ate there again.

It was the same story all over New Jersey, in bars, bowling alleys, diners, places to live. I was always being forced to leave, silently, or with mutual imprecations. I very shortly became notorious and children giggled behind me when I passed and their elders whispered or shouted — they really believed that I was mad. And it did begin to work on my mind, of course; I began to be afraid to go anywhere and to compensate for this I went places to which I really should not have gone and where, God knows, I had no desire to be. My reputation in town naturally enhanced my reputation at work and my working day became one long series of acrobatics designed to keep me out of trouble. I cannot say that these acrobatics succeeded. It began to seem that the machinery of the organization I worked for was turning over, day and night, with but one aim: to eject me. I was fired once, and contrived, with the aid of a friend from New York, to get back on the payroll; was fired again, and bounced back again. It took a while to fire me for the third time, but the third time took. There were no loopholes anywhere. There was not even any way of getting back inside the gates.

That year in New Jersey lives in my mind as though it were the year during which, having an unsuspected predilection for it, I first contracted some dread, chronic disease, the unfailing symptom of which is a kind of blind fever, a pounding in the skull and fire in the bowels. Once this disease is contracted, one can never be really carefree again, for the fever, without an instant's warning, can recur at any moment. It can wreck more important things than race relations. There is not a Negro alive who does not have this rage in his blood — one has the choice, merely, of living with it consciously or surrendering to it. As for me, this fever has recurred in me, and does, and will until the day I die.

My last night in New Jersey, a white friend from New York took me to the nearest big town, Trenton, to go to the movies and have a few drinks. As it turned out, he also saved me from, at the very least, a violent whipping. Almost every detail of that night stands out very clearly in my memory. I even remember the name of the movie we saw because its title impressed me as being so patly ironical. It was a movie about the German occupation of France, starring Maureen O'Hara and Charles Laughton and called *This Land Is Mine.* I remember the name of the diner we walked into when the movie ended: it was the "American Diner." When we walked in the counterman asked what we wanted and I remember answering with the casual sharpness which had become my habit: "We want a hamburger and a cup of coffee; what do you think we want?" I do not know why, after a year of such rebuffs, I so completely failed to anticipate his answer, which was, of course, "We don't serve Negroes here." This reply failed to discompose me, at least for the moment. I made some sardonic comment about the name of the diner and we walked out into the streets.

This was the time of what was called the "brown-out," when the lights in all American cities were very dim. When we re-entered the streets something happened to me which had the force of an optical illusion, or a nightmare. The streets were very crowded and I was facing north. People were moving in every direction but it seemed to me, in that instant, that all of the people I could see, and many more than that, were moving toward me, against me, and that everyone was white. I remember how their faces gleamed. And I felt, like a physical sensation, a *click* at the nape of my neck as though some interior string connecting my head to my body had been cut. I began to walk. I heard my friend call after me, but I ignored him. Heaven only knows what was going on in his mind, but he had the good sense not to touch me — I don't know what would have happened if he had — and to keep me in sight. I don't know what was going on in my mind, either; I certainly had no conscious plan. I wanted to do something to crush these white faces, which were crushing me. I walked for perhaps a block or two until I came to an enormous, glittering, and fashionable restaurant in which I knew not even the intercession of the Virgin would cause me to be served. I pushed through the doors and took the first vacant seat I saw, at a table for two, and waited.

I do not know how long I waited and I rather wonder, until today, what I could possibly have looked like. Whatever I looked like, I frightened the waitress who shortly appeared, and the moment she appeared all of my fury flowed towards her. I hated her for her white face, and for her great, astounded, frightened eyes. I felt that if she found a black man so frightening I would make her fright worthwhile.

She did not ask me what I wanted, but repeated, as though she had learned it somewhere, "We don't serve Negroes here." She did not say it with the blunt, derisive hostility to which I had grown so accustomed, but, rather, with a note of apology in her voice, and fear. This made me colder and more murderous than ever. I felt I had to do something with my hands. I wanted her to come close enough for me to get her neck between my hands.

So I pretended not to have understood her, hoping to draw her closer. And she did step a very short step closer, with her pencil poised incongruously over her pad, and repeated the formula: ". . . don't serve Negroes here."

Somehow, with the repetition of that phrase, which was already ringing in my head like a thousand bells of a nightmare, I realized that she would never come any closer and that I would have to strike from a distance. There was nothing on the table but an ordinary watermug half full of water, and I picked this up and hurled it with all my strength at her. She ducked and it missed her and shattered against the mirror behind the bar. And, with that sound, my frozen blood abruptly thawed, I returned from wherever I had been, I *saw*, for the first time, the restaurant, the people with their mouths open, already, as it seemed to me, rising as one man, and I realized what I had done, and where I was, and I was frightened. I rose and began running for the door. A round, potbellied man grabbed me by the nape of the neck just as I reached the doors and began to beat me about the face. I kicked him and got loose and ran into the streets. My friend whispered, "*Run!*" and I ran.

My friend stayed outside the restaurant long enough to misdirect my pursuers and the police, who arrived, he told me, at once. I do not know what I said to him when he came to my room that night. I could not have said much. I felt, in the oddest, most awful way, that I had somehow betrayed him. I lived it over and over and over again, the way one relives an automobile accident after it has happened and one finds oneself alone and safe. I could not get over two facts, both equally difficult for the imagination to grasp, and one was that I could have been murdered. But the other was that I had been ready to commit murder. I saw nothing very clearly but I did see this: that my life, my *real* life, was in danger, and not from anything other people might do but from the hatred I carried in my own heart.

I had returned home around the second week in June — in great haste because it seemed that my father's death and my mother's confinement were both but a matter of hours. In the case of my mother, it soon became clear that she had simply made a miscalculation. This had always been her tendency and I don't believe that a single one of us arrived in the world, or has since arrived anywhere else, on time. But none of us dawdled so intolerably about the business of being born as did my baby sister. We sometimes amused ourselves, during those endless, stifling weeks, by picturing the baby sitting within in the safe, warm dark, bitterly regretting the necessity of becoming a part of our chaos and stubbornly putting it off as long as possible. I understood her perfectly and congratulated her on showing such good sense so soon. Death, however, sat as purposefully at my father's bedside as life stirred within my mother's womb and it was harder to understand why he so lingered in that long shadow. It seemed that he had bent, and for a long time, too, all of his energies towards dying. Now death was ready for him, but my father held back.

All of Harlem, indeed, seemed to be infected by waiting. I had never before known it to be so violently still. Racial tensions throughout this country were exacerbated during the early years of the war, partly because the labor market brought together hundreds of thousands of ill-prepared people and partly because Negro soldiers, regardless of where they were born, received their military training in the South. What happened in defense plants and army camps had repercussions, naturally, in every Negro ghetto. The situation in Harlem had grown bad enough for clergymen, policemen, educators, politicians, and social workers to assert in one breath that there was no "crime wave" and to offer, in the very next breath, suggestions as to how to combat it. These suggestions always seemed to involve playgrounds, despite the fact that racial skirmishes were occurring in the playgrounds, too. Playground or not, crime wave or not, the Harlem police force had been augmented in March, and the unrest grew — perhaps, in fact, partly as a result of the ghetto's instinctive hatred of policemen. Perhaps the most revealing news item, out of the steady parade of reports of muggings, stabbings, shootings, assaults, gang wars, and accusations of police brutality, is the item concerning six Negro girls who set upon a white girl in the subway because, as they all too accurately put it, she was stepping on their toes. Indeed she was, all over the nation.

I had never before been so aware of policemen, on foot, on horseback, on corners, everywhere, always two by two. Nor had I ever been so aware of small knots of people. They were on stoops and on corners and in doorways, and what was striking about them, I think, was that they did not seem to be talking. Never, when I passed these groups, did the usual sound of a curse or a laugh ring out and neither did there seem to be any hum of gossip. There was certainly, on the other hand, occurring between them communication extraordinarily intense. Another thing that was striking was the unexpected diversity of the people who made up these groups. Usually, for example, one would see a group of sharpies standing on the street corner, jiving the passing chicks; or a group of older men, usually, for some reason, in the vicinity of a barber shop, discussing baseball scores, or the numbers, or making rather chilling observations about women they had known. Women, in a general way, tended to be seen less often together — unless they were church women, or very young girls, or prostitutes met together for an unprofessional instant. But that summer I saw the strangest combinations: large, respectable, churchly matrons standing on the stoops or the corners with their hair tied up, together with a girl in sleazy satin whose face bore the marks of gin and the razor, or heavy-set, abrupt, no-nonsense older men, in company with the most disreputable and fanatical "race" men, or these same "race" men with the sharpies, or these sharpies with the churchly women. Seventh Day Adventists and Methodists and Spiritualists seemed to be hobnobbing with Holyrollers and they were all, alike, entangled with the most flagrant disbelievers; something heavy in their stance seemed to indicate that they had all, incredibly, seen a common vision, and on each face there seemed to be the same strange, bitter shadow.

The churchly women and the matter-of-fact, no-nonsense men had children in the Army. The sleazy girls they talked to had lovers there, the sharpies and the "race" men had friends and brothers there. It would have demanded an unquestioning patriotism, happily as uncommon in this country as it is undesirable, for these people not to have been disturbed by the bitter letters they received, by the newspaper stories they read, not to have been enraged by the posters, then to be found all over New York, which described the Japanese as "yellow-bellied Japs." It was only the "race" men, to be sure, who spoke ceaselessly of being revenged — how this vengeance was to be exacted was not clear — for the indignities and dangers suffered by Negro boys in uniform; but everybody felt a directionless, hopeless bitterness, as well as that panic which can scarcely be suppressed when one knows that a human being one loves is beyond one's reach, and in danger. This helplessness and this gnawing uneasiness does something, at length, to even the toughest mind. Perhaps the best way to sum all this up is to say that the people I knew felt, mainly, a peculiar kind of relief when they knew that their boys were being shipped out of the South, to do battle overseas. It was, perhaps, like feeling that the most dangerous part of a dangerous journey had been passed and that now, even if death should come, it would come with honor and without the complicity of their countrymen. Such a death would be, in short, a fact with which one could hope to live.

It was on the 28th of July, which I believe was a Wednesday, that I visited my father for the first time during his illness and for the last time in his life. The moment I saw him I knew why I had put off this visit so long. I had told my mother that I did not want to see him because I hated him. But this was not true. It was only that I *had* hated him and I wanted to hold on to this hatred. I did not want to look on him as a ruin: it was not a ruin I had hated. I imagine that one of the reasons people cling to their hates so stubbornly is because they sense, once hate is gone, that they will be forced to deal with pain.

We traveled out to him, his older sister and myself, to what seemed to be the very end of a very Long Island. It was hot and dusty and we wrangled, my aunt and I, all the way out, over the fact that I had recently begun to smoke and, as she said, to give myself airs. But I knew that she wrangled with me because she could not bear to face the fact of her brother's dying. Neither could I endure the reality of her despair, her unstated bafflement as to what had happened to her brother's life, and her own. So we wrangled and I smoked and from time to time she fell into a heavy reverie. Covertly, I watched her face, which was the face of an old woman; it had fallen in, the eyes were sunken and lightless; soon she would be dying, too.

In my childhood — it had not been so long ago — I had thought her beautiful. She had been quick-witted and quick-moving and very generous with all the children and each of her visits had been an event. At one time one of my brothers and myself had thought of running away to live with her. Now she could no longer produce out of her handbag some unexpected and yet familiar delight. She made me feel pity and revulsion and fear. It was awful to realize that she no longer caused me to feel affection. The closer we came to the hospital the more querulous she became and at the same time, naturally, grew more dependent on me. Between pity and guilt and fear I began to feel that there was another me trapped in my skull like a jack-in-the-box who might escape my control at any moment and fill the air with screaming.

She began to cry the moment we entered the room and she saw him lying there, all shriveled and still, like a little black monkey. The great, gleaming apparatus which fed him and would have compelled him to be still even if he had been able to move brought to mind, not beneficence, but torture; the tubes entering his arm made me think of pictures I had seen when a child, of Gulliver, tied down by the pygmies on that island. My aunt wept and wept; there was a whistling sound in my father's throat; nothing was said; he could not speak. I wanted to take his hand, to say something. But I do not know what I could have said, even if he could have heard me. He was not really in that room with us; he had at last really embarked on his journey; and though my aunt told me that he said he was going to meet Jesus, I did not hear anything except that whistling in his throat. The doctor came back and we left, into that unbearable train again, and home. In the morning came the telegram saying that he was dead. Then the house was suddenly full of relatives, friends, hysteria, and confusion and I quickly left my mother and the children to the care of those impressive women, who, in Negro communities at least, automatically appear at times of bereavement armed with lotions, proverbs, and patience, and an ability to cook. I went downtown. By the time I returned, later the same day, my mother had been carried to the hospital and the baby had been born.

For my father's funeral I had nothing black to wear and this posed a nagging problem all day long. It was one of those problems, simple, or impossible of solution, to which the mind insanely clings in order to avoid the mind's real trouble. I spent most of that day at the downtown apartment of a girl I knew, celebrating my birthday with whiskey and wondering what to wear that night. When planning a birthday celebration one naturally does not expect that it will be up against competition from a funeral and this girl had anticipated taking me out that night, for a big dinner and a nightclub afterwards. Sometime during the course of that long day we decided that we would go out anyway, when my father's funeral service was over. I imagine I decided it, since, as the funeral hour approached, it became clearer and clearer to me that I would not know what to do with myself when it was over. The girl, stifling her very lively concern as to the possible effects of the whiskey on one of my father's chief mourners, concentrated on being conciliatory and practically helpful. She found a black shirt for me somewhere and ironed it and, dressed in the darkest pants and jacket I owned, and slightly drunk, I made my way to my father's funeral.

The chapel was full, but not packed, and very quiet. There were, mainly, my father's relatives, and his children, and here and there I saw faces I had not seen since childhood, the faces of my father's one-time friends. They were very dark and solemn now, seeming somehow to suggest that they had known all along that something like this would happen. Chief among the mourners was my aunt, who had quarreled with my father all his life; by which I do not mean to suggest that her mourning was insincere or that she had not loved him. I suppose that she was one of the few people in the world who had, and their incessant quarreling proved precisely the strength of the tie that bound them. The only other person in the world, as far as I knew, whose relationship to my father rivaled my aunt's in depth was my mother, who was not there.

It seemed to me, of course, that it was a very long funeral. But it was, if anything, a rather shorter funeral than most, nor, since there were no overwhelming, uncontrollable expressions of grief, could it be called — if I dare to use the word — successful. The minister who preached my father's funeral sermon was one of the few my father had still been seeing as he neared his end. He presented to us in his sermon a man whom none of us had ever seen — a man thoughtful, patient, and forbearing, a Christian inspiration to all who knew him, and a model for his children. And no doubt the children, in their disturbed and guilty state, were almost ready to believe this; he had been remote enough to be anything and, anyway, the shock of the incontrovertible, that it was really our father lying up there in that casket, prepared the mind for anything. His sister moaned and this grief-stricken moaning was taken as corroboration. The other faces held a dark, noncommittal thoughtfulness. This was not the man they had known, but they had scarcely expected to be confronted with *him;* this was, in a sense deeper than questions of fact, the man they had not known, and the man they had not known may have been the real one. The real man, whoever he had been, had suffered and now he was dead: this was all that was sure and all that mattered now. Every man in the chapel hoped that when his hour came he, too, would be eulogized, which is to say forgiven, and that all of his lapses, greeds, errors, and strayings from the truth would be invested with coherence and looked upon with charity. This was perhaps the last thing human beings could give each other and it was what they demanded, after all, of the Lord. Only the Lord saw the midnight tears; only He was present when one of His children, moaning and wringing hands, paced up and down the room. When one slapped one's child in anger, the recoil in the heart reverberated through heaven and became part of the pain of the universe. And when the children were hungry and sullen and distrustful and one watched them, daily, growing wilder, and further away, and running headlong into danger, it was the Lord who knew what the charged heart endured as the strap was laid to the backside; the Lord alone who knew what one *would* have said if one had had, like the Lord, the gift of the living word. It was the Lord who knew of the impossibility every parent in that room faced: how to prepare the child for the day when the child would be despised and how to *create* in the child — by what means? — a stronger antidote to this poison than one had found for oneself. The avenues, side streets, bars, billiard halls, hospitals, police stations, and even the playgrounds of Harlem — not to mention the houses of correction, the jails, and the morgue — testified to the potency of the poison while remaining silent as to the efficacy of whatever antidote, irresistibly raising the question of whether or not such an antidote existed; raising, which was worse, the question of whether or not an antidote was desirable; perhaps poison should be fought with poison. With these several schisms in the mind and with more terrors in the heart than could be named, it was better not to judge the man who had gone down under an impossible burden. It was better to remember: *Thou knowest this man's fall; but thou knowest not his wrassling.*

While the preacher talked and I watched the children — years of changing their diapers, scrubbing them, slapping them, taking them to school, and scolding them had had the perhaps inevitable result of making me love them, though I am not sure I knew this then — my mind was busily breaking out with a rash of disconnected impressions. Snatches of popular songs, indecent jokes, bits of books I had read, movie sequences, faces, voices, political issues — I thought I was going mad; all these impressions suspended, as it were, in the solution of the faint nausea produced in me by the heat and liquor. For a moment I had the impression that my alcoholic breath, inefficiently disguised with chewing gum, filled the entire chapel. Then someone began singing one of my father's favorite songs and, abruptly, I was with him, sitting on his knee, in the hot, enormous, crowded church which was the first church we attended. It was the Abyssinia Baptist Church on 138th Street. We had not gone there long. With this image, a host of others came. I had forgotten, in the rage of my growing up, how proud my father had been of me when I was little. Apparently, I had had a voice and my father had liked to show me off before the members of the church. I had forgotten what he had looked like when he was pleased but now I remembered that he had always been grinning with pleasure when my solos ended. I even remembered certain expressions on his face when he teased my mother — had he loved her? I would never know. And when had it all begun to change? For now it seemed that he had not always been cruel. I remembered being taken for a haircut and scraping my knee on the footrest of the barber's chair and I remembered my father's face as he soothed my crying and applied the stinging iodine. Then I remembered our fights, fights which had been of the worst possible kind because my technique had been silence.

I remembered the one time in all our life together when we had really spoken to each other.

It was on a Sunday and it must have been shortly before I left home. We were walking, just the two of us, in our usual silence, to or from church. I was in high school and had been doing a lot of writing and I was, at about this time, the editor of the high school magazine. But I had also been a Young Minister and had been preaching from the pulpit. Lately, I had been taking fewer engagements and preached as rarely as possible. It was said in the church, quite truthfully, that I was "cooling off."

My father asked me abruptly, "You'd rather write than preach, wouldn't you?"

I was astonished at his question — because it was a real question. I answered, "Yes."

That was all we said. It was awful to remember that that was all we had *ever* said.

The casket now was opened and the mourners were being led up the aisle to look for the last time on the deceased. The assumption was that the family was too overcome with grief to be allowed to make this journey alone and I watched while my aunt was led to the casket and, muffled in black, and shaking, led back to her seat. I disapproved of forcing the children to look on their dead father, considering that the shock of his death, or, more truthfully, the shock of death as a reality, was already a little more than a child could bear, but my judgment in this matter had been overruled and there they were, bewildered and frightened and very small, being led, one by one, to the casket. But there is also something very gallant about children at such moments. It has something to do with their silence and gravity and with the fact that one cannot help them. Their legs, somehow, seem *exposed*, so that it is at once incredible and terribly clear that their legs are all they have to hold them up.

I had not wanted to go to the casket myself and I certainly had not wished to be led there, but there was no way of avoiding either of these forms. One of the deacons led me up and I looked on my father's face. I cannot say that it looked like him at all. His blackness had been equivocated by powder and there was no suggestion in that casket of what his power had or could have been. He was simply an old man dead, and it was hard to believe that he had ever given anyone either joy or pain. Yet, his life filled that room. Further up the avenue his wife was holding his newborn child. Life and death so close together, and love and hatred, and right and wrong, said something to me which I did not want to hear concerning man, concerning the life of man.

After the funeral, while I was downtown desperately celebrating my birthday, a Negro soldier, in the lobby of the Hotel Braddock, got into a fight with a white policeman over a Negro girl. Negro girls, white policemen, in or out of uniform, and Negro males — in or out of uniform — were part of the furniture of the lobby of the Hotel Braddock and this was certainly not the first time such an incident had occurred. It was destined, however, to receive an unprecedented publicity, for the fight between the policeman and the soldier ended with the shooting of the soldier. Rumor, flowing immediately to the streets outside, stated that the soldier had been shot in the back, an instantaneous and revealing invention, and that the soldier had died protecting a Negro woman. The facts were somewhat different — for example, the soldier had not been shot in the back, and was not dead, and the girl seems to have been as dubious a symbol of womanhood as her white counterpart in Georgia usually is, but no one was interested in the facts. They preferred the invention because this invention expressed and corroborated their hates and fears so perfectly. It is just as well to remember that people are always doing this. Perhaps many of those legends, including Christianity, to which the world clings began their conquest of the world with just some such concerted surrender to distortion. The effect, in Harlem, of this particular legend was like the effect of a lit match in a tin of gasoline. The mob gathered before the doors of the Hotel Braddock simply began to swell and to spread in every direction, and Harlem exploded.

The mob did not cross the ghetto lines. It would have been easy, for example, to have gone over Morningside Park on the west side or to have crossed the Grand Central railroad tracks at 125th Street on the east side, to wreak havoc in white neighborhoods. The mob seems to have been mainly interested in something more potent and real than the white face, that is, in white power, and the principal damage done during the riot of the summer of 1943 was to white business establishments in Harlem. It might have been a far bloodier story, of course, if, at the hour the riot began, these establishments had still been open. From the Hotel Braddock the mob fanned out, east and west along 125th Street, and for the entire length of Lenox, Seventh, and Eighth avenues. Along each of these avenues, and along each major side street — 116th, 125th, 135th, and so on — bars, stores, pawnshops, restaurants, even little luncheonettes had been smashed open and entered and looted — looted, it might be added, with more haste than efficiency. The shelves really looked as though a bomb had struck them. Cans of beans and soup and dog food, along with toilet paper, corn flakes, sardines and milk tumbled every which way, and abandoned cash registers and cases of beer leaned crazily out of the splintered windows and were strewn along the avenues. Sheets, blankets, and clothing of every description formed a kind of path, as though people had dropped them while running. I truly had not realized that Harlem *had* so many stores until I saw them all smashed open; the first time the word *wealth* ever entered my mind in relation to Harlem was when I saw it scattered in the streets. But one's first, incongruous impression of plenty was countered immediately by an impression of waste. None of this was doing anybody any good. It would have been better to have left the plate glass as it had been and the goods lying in the stores.

It would have been better, but it would also have been intolerable, for Harlem had needed something to smash. To smash something is the ghetto's chronic need. Most of the time it is the members of the ghetto who smash each other, and themselves. But as long as the ghetto walls are standing there will always come a moment when these outlets do not work. That summer, for example, it was not enough to get into a fight on Lenox Avenue, or curse out one's cronies in the barber shops. If ever, indeed, the violence which fills Harlem's churches, pool halls, and bars erupts outward in a more direct fashion, Harlem and its citizens are likely to vanish in an apocalyptic flood. That this is not likely to happen is due to a great many reasons, most hidden and powerful among them the Negro's real relation to the white American. This relation prohibits, simply, anything as uncomplicated and satisfactory as pure hatred. In order really to hate white people, one has to blot so much out of the mind — and the heart — that this hatred itself becomes an exhausting and self-destructive pose. But this does not mean, on the other hand, that love comes easily: the white world is too powerful, too complacent, too ready with gratuitous humiliation, and, above all, too ignorant and too innocent for that. One is absolutely forced to make perpetual qualifications and one's own reactions are always canceling each other out. It is this, really, which has driven so many people mad, both white and black. One is always in the position of having to decide between amputation and gangrene. Amputation is swift but time may prove that the amputation was not necessary — or one may delay the amputation too long. Gangrene is slow, but it is impossible to be sure that one is reading one's symptoms right. The idea of going through life as a cripple is more than one can bear, and equally unbearable is the risk of swelling up slowly, in agony, with poison. And the trouble, finally, is that the risks are real even if the choices do not exist.

"But as for me and my house," my father had said, "we will serve the Lord." I wondered, as we drove him to his resting place, what this line had meant for him. I had heard him preach it many times. I had preached it once myself, proudly giving it an interpretation different from my father's. Now the whole thing came back to me, as though my father and I were on our way to Sunday school and I were memorizing the golden text: *And if it seem evil unto you to serve the Lord, choose you this day whom you will serve; whether the gods which your fathers served that were on the other side of the flood, or the gods of the Amorites, in whose land ye dwell: but as for me and my house, we will serve the Lord.* I suspected in these familiar lines a meaning which had never been there for me before. All of my father's texts and songs, which I had decided were meaningless, were arranged before me at his death like empty bottles, waiting to hold the meaning which life would give them for me. This was his legacy: nothing is ever escaped. That bleakly memorable morning I hated the unbelievable streets and the Negroes and whites who had, equally, made them that way. But I knew that it was folly, as my father would have said, this bitterness was folly. It was necessary to hold on to the things that mattered. The dead man mattered, the new life mattered; blackness and whiteness did not matter; to believe that they did was to acquiesce in one's own destruction. Hatred, which could destroy so much, never failed to destroy the man who hated and this was an immutable law.

It began to seem that one would have to hold in the mind forever two ideas which seemed to be in opposition. The first idea was acceptance, the acceptance, totally without rancor, of life as it is, and men as they are: in the light of this idea, it goes without saying that injustice is a commonplace. But this did not mean that one could be complacent, for the second idea was of equal power: that one must never, in one's own life, accept these injustices as commonplace but must fight them with all one's strength. This fight begins, however, in the heart and it now had been laid to my charge to keep my own heart free of hatred and despair. This intimation made my heart heavy and, now that my father was irrecoverable, I wished that he had been beside me so that I could have searched his face for the answers which only the future would give me now.

FOR DISCUSSION

1. Describe the relationship between Baldwin and his father. How did their attitudes towards race affect this relationship? Baldwin says that the hostility between his father and himself is typical of America, where "the second generation has no time to talk to the first." Do you agree?
2. Describe the events in the fashionable restaurant. What caused Baldwin to act the way he did?
3. Baldwin says, "to smash something is the ghetto's chronic need." Do you agree that riots like the one he describes are inevitable?
4. In this essay, Baldwin describes two unhealthy relationships: that between father and son, and that between blacks and whites. How are these two relationships similar?

Civil Rights

Martin Luther King, Jr.

(*1929–1968*)

Awarded the Nobel Peace Prize for his efforts as a non-violent civil rights leader, Martin Luther King, Jr. was one of America's most outstanding black spokesmen. Educated at Morehouse College, Crozer Theological Seminary, Boston University, and the University of Chicago, King held both Ph.D. and D.D. degrees. King ended bus segregation in Montgomery, Alabama, through his carefully planned boycott of buses in that city. The organizer of the Southern Christian Leadership Conference, he staged mass demonstrations and carried his crusade for equality throughout the South. He made Birmingham a battleground for civil rights and was jailed for leading the movement against discrimination and injustice. In his famous letter written from prison, he defended his actions: ". . . we must see the need of having nonviolent gadflies to create the kind of tension in society that will help men rise from the dark depths of prejudice and racism to the majestic heights of understanding and brotherhood."

In 1963, King led the famous March on Washington; his dramatic efforts anticipated the Civil Rights Act passed a year later. King organized voter registration drives in Alabama and led a march from Selma to Montgomery in 1965. In 1966, he focused his concern upon the slums of Chicago to call attention to de facto segregation in the North. In April, 1968, Dr. King was assassinated.

102

I Have a Dream

Five score years ago, a great American, in whose symbolic shadow we stand, signed the Emancipation Proclamation. This momentous decree came as a great beacon light of hope to millions of Negro slaves who had been seared in the flames of withering injustice. It came as a joyous daybreak to end the long night of captivity.

But one hundred years later, we must face the tragic fact that the Negro is still not free. One hundred years later, the life of the Negro is still sadly crippled by the manacles of segregation and the chains of discrimination. One hundred years later, the Negro lives on a lonely island of poverty in the midst of a vast ocean of material prosperity. One hundred years later, the Negro is still languished in the corners of American society and finds himself an exile in his own land. So we have come here today to dramatize an appalling condition.

In a sense we have come to our nation's capital to cash a check. When the architects of our republic wrote the magnificent words of the Constitution and the Declaration of Independence, they were signing a promissory note to which every American was to fall heir. This note was a promise that all men would be guaranteed the unalienable rights of life, liberty, and the pursuit of happiness.

It is obvious today that America has defaulted on this promissory note insofar as her citizens of color are concerned. Instead of honoring this sacred obligation, America has given the Negro people a bad check, a check which has come back marked "insufficient funds." But we refuse to believe that the bank of justice is bankrupt. We refuse to believe that there are insufficient funds in the great vaults of opportunity of this nation. So we have come to cash this check — a check that will give us upon demand the riches of freedom and the security of justice. We have also come to this hallowed spot to remind America of the fierce urgency of *now*. This is no time to engage in the luxury of cooling off or to take the tranquilizing drug of gradualism. *Now* is the time to make real the promises of democracy. *Now* is the time to rise from the dark and desolate valley of segregation to the sunlit path of racial justice. *Now* is the time to open the doors of opportunity to all of God's children. *Now* is the time to lift our nation from the quicksands of racial injustice to the solid rock of brotherhood.

It would be fatal for the nation to overlook the urgency of the moment and to underestimate the determination of the Negro. This sweltering summer of the Negro's legitimate discontent will not pass until there is an invigorating autumn of freedom and equality. Nineteen sixty-three is not an end, but a beginning. Those who hope that the Negro needed to blow off steam and will now be content will have a rude awakening if the nation returns to business as usual. There will be neither rest nor tranquility in America until the Negro is granted his citizenship rights. The whirlwinds of revolt will continue to shake the foundations of our nation until the bright day of justice emerges.

But there is something that I must say to my people who stand on the warm threshold which leads into the palace of justice. In the process of gaining our rightful place we must not be guilty of wrongful deeds. Let us not seek to satisfy our thirst for freedom by drinking from the cup of bitterness and hatred. We must forever conduct our struggle on the high plane of dignity and discipline. We must not allow our creative protest to degenerate into physical violence. Again and again we must rise to the majestic heights of meeting physical force with soul force. The marvelous new militancy which has engulfed the Negro community must not lead us to a distrust of all white people, for many of our white brothers, as evidenced by their presence here today, have come to realize that their destiny is tied up with our destiny and their freedom is inextricably bound to our freedom. We cannot walk alone.

And as we walk, we must make the pledge that we shall march ahead. We cannot turn back. There are those who are asking the devotees of civil rights, "When will you be satisfied?" We can never be satisfied as long as the Negro is the victim of the unspeakable horrors of police brutality. We can never be satisfied as long as our bodies, heavy with the fatigue of travel, cannot gain lodging in the motels of the highways and the hotels of the cities. We cannot be satisfied as long as the Negro's basic mobility is from a smaller ghetto to a larger one. We can never be satisfied as long as a Negro in Mississippi cannot vote and a Negro in New York believes he has nothing for which to vote. No, no, we are not satisfied, and we will not be satisfied until justice rolls down like waters and righteousness like a mighty stream.

I am not unmindful that some of you have come here out of great trials and tribulations. Some of you have come fresh from narrow jail cells. Some of you have come from areas where your quest for freedom left you battered by the storms of persecution and staggered by the winds of police brutality. You have been the veterans of creative suffering. Continue to work with the faith that unearned suffering is redemptive.

Go back to Mississippi, go back to Alabama, go back to South Carolina, go back to Georgia, go back to Louisiana, go back to the slums and the ghettos of our Northern cities, knowing that somehow this situation can and will be changed. Let us not wallow in the valley of despair.

I say to you today, my friends, that in spite of the difficulties and frustrations of the moment I still have a dream. It is a dream deeply rooted in the American dream.

I have a dream that one day this nation will rise up and live out the true meaning of its creed: "We hold these truths to be self-evident; that all men are created equal."

I have a dream that one day on the red hills of Georgia the sons of former slaves and the sons of former slaveowners will be able to sit down together at the table of brotherhood.

I have a dream that one day even the state of Mississippi, a desert state sweltering with the heat of injustice and oppression, will be transformed into an oasis of freedom and justice.

I have a dream that my four little children will one day live in a nation where they will not be judged by the color of their skin but by the content of their character.

I have a dream today.

I have a dream that one day the state of Alabama, whose governor's lips are presently dripping with the words of interposition and nullification, will be transformed into a situation where little black boys and black girls will be able to join hands with little white boys and white girls and walk together as sisters and brothers.

I have a dream today.

I have a dream that one day every valley shall be exalted, every hill and mountain shall be made low, the rough places will be made plain, and the crooked places will be made straight, and the glory of the Lord shall be revealed, and all flesh shall see it together.

This is our hope. This is the faith with which I return to the South. With this faith we will be able to hew out of the mountain of despair a stone of hope. With this faith we will be able to transform the jangling discords of our nation into a beautiful symphony of brotherhood. With this faith we will be able to work together, to pray together, to struggle together, to go to jail together, to stand up for freedom together, knowing that we will be free one day.

This will be the day when all of God's children will be able to sing with new meaning

> My country, 'tis of thee
> Sweet land of liberty,
>   Of thee I sing:
> Land where my fathers died,
> Land of the pilgrims' pride,
> From every mountain-side
>   Let freedom ring.

And if America is to be a great nation this must become true. So let freedom ring from the prodigious hilltops of New Hampshire. Let freedom ring from the mighty mountains of New York. Let freedom ring from the heightening Alleghenies of Pennsylvania!

Let freedom ring from the curvaceous peaks of California!

Let freedom ring from the snowcapped Rockies of Colorado!

But not only that; let freedom ring from Stone Mountain of Georgia!

Let freedom ring from Lookout Mountain of Tennessee!

Let freedom ring from every hill and molehill of Mississippi.

From every mountainside, let freedom ring.

When we let freedom ring, when we let it ring from every village and every hamlet, from every state and every city, we will be able to speed up that day when all of God's children, black men and white men, Jews and Gentiles, Protestants and Catholics, will be able to join hands and sing in the words of the old Negro spiritual, "Free at last; free at last! Thank God almighty, we are free at last!"

FOR DISCUSSION

1. Dr. King's famous speech is a very strong plea for nonviolence. He even speaks of "creative suffering," and claims that "unearned suffering is redemptive." Do you agree with his philosophy?
2. This speech, which Martin Luther King delivered in 1963, is profoundly optimistic. On the basis of all that has happened since, do you think his optimism was justified?
3. In the conclusion of his speech, Dr. King argues strongly for integration. Do you think that full integration can be achieved? Do you think that it is a desirable goal?

Anne Moody

(1941–   )

Anne Moody, the daughter of a sharecropper in Wilkinson County, Mississippi, spent her early years in extreme poverty. Miss Moody was only nine when she went to work as a maid. Her first realization that being poor and black could be an actual threat came when Emmet Till, a fourteen-year-old Chicago black youth visiting in Mississippi, was murdered for "getting out of line with a white woman."

Miss Moody was determined to go to college, so she worked in Baton Rouge and New Orleans summers during high school to save money. She had been an honor student in school, but it was her ability as a basketball player which won her a scholarship to Natchez Junior College, a Baptist college for black students. After two years at Natchez, Miss Moody transferred to Tougaloo College in Jackson, Mississippi.

At Tougaloo she became involved in the Mississippi civil rights movement; she also became an active member of the Student Nonviolent Coordinating Committee. She and other SNCC workers spent the summer of 1962 in Greenwood, Mississippi, canvassing black people for voter registration. Of that summer she says, "I could feel myself beginning to change. For the first time I began to think something would be done about whites killing, beating, and misusing Negroes. I knew I was going to be a part of whatever happened." The following selection is taken from Miss Moody's *Coming of Age in Mississippi.*

The Movement

I had counted on graduating in the spring of 1963, but as it turned out, I couldn't because some of my credits still had to be cleared with Natchez College. A year before, this would have seemed like a terrible disaster, but now I hardly even felt disappointed. I had a good excuse to stay on campus for the summer and work with the Movement, and this was what I really wanted to do. I couldn't go home again anyway, and I couldn't go to New Orleans — I didn't have money enough for bus fare.

During my senior year at Tougaloo, my family hadn't sent me one penny. I had only the small amount of money I had earned at Maple Hill. I couldn't afford to eat at school or live in the dorms, so I had gotten permission to move off campus. I had to prove that I could finish school, even if I had to go hungry every day. I knew Raymond and Miss Pearl were just waiting to see me drop out. But something happened to me as I got more and more involved in the Movement. It no longer seemed important to prove anything. I had found something outside myself that gave meaning to my life.

I had become very friendly with my social science professor, John Salter, who was in charge of NAACP activities on campus. All during the year, while the NAACP conducted a boycott of the downtown stores in Jackson, I had been one of Salter's most faithful canvassers and church speakers. During the last week of school, he told me that sit-in demonstrations were about to start in Jackson and that he wanted me to be the spokesman for a team that would sit-in at Woolworth's lunch counter. The two other

109

demonstrators would be classmates of mine, Memphis and Pearlena. Pearlena was a dedicated NAACP worker, but Memphis had not been very involved in the Movement on campus. It seemed that the organization had had a rough time finding students who were in a position to go to jail. I had nothing to lose one way or the other. Around ten o'clock the morning of the demonstrations, NAACP headquarters alerted the news services. As a result, the police department was also informed, but neither the policemen nor the newsmen knew exactly where or when the demonstrations would start. They stationed themselves along Capitol Street and waited.

To divert attention from the sit-in at Woolworth's, the picketing started at J. C. Penney's a good fifteen minutes before. The pickets were allowed to walk up and down in front of the store three or four times before they were arrested. At exactly 11 A.M., Pearlena, Memphis, and I entered Woolworth's from the rear entrance. We separated as soon as we stepped into the store, and made small purchases from various counters. Pearlena had given Memphis her watch. He was to let us know when it was 11:14. At 11:14 we were to join him near the lunch counter and at exactly 11:15 we were to take seats at it.

Seconds before 11:15 we were occupying three seats at the previously segregated Woolworth's lunch counter. In the beginning the waitresses seemed to ignore us, as if they really didn't know what was going on. Our waitress walked past us a couple of times before she noticed we had started to write our own orders down and realized we wanted service. She asked us what we wanted. We began to read to her from our order slips. She told us that we would be served at the back counter, which was for Negroes.

"We would like to be served here," I said.

The waitress started to repeat what she had said, then stopped in the middle of the sentence. She turned the lights out behind the counter, and she and the other waitresses almost ran to the back of the store, deserting all their white customers. I guess they thought that violence would start immediately after the whites at the counter realized what was going on. There were five or six other people at the counter. A couple of them just got up and walked away. A girl sitting next to me finished her banana split before leaving. A middle-aged white woman who had not yet been served rose from her seat and came over to us. "I'd like to stay here with you," she said, "but my husband is waiting."

The newsmen came in just as she was leaving. They must have discovered what was going on shortly after some of the people began to leave the store. One of the newsmen ran behind the woman who spoke to us and asked her to identify herself. She refused to give her name, but said she was a native of Vicksburg and a former resident of California. When asked why she had said what she had said to us, she replied, "I am in sympathy with the Negro movement." By this time a crowd of cameramen and reporters had gathered around us taking pictures and asking questions, such as Where were we from? Why did we sit-in? What organization sponsored it? Were we students? From what school? How were we classified?

I told them that we were all students at Tougaloo College, that we were represented by no particular organization, and that we planned to stay there even after the store closed. "All we want is service," was my reply to one of them. After they had finished probing for about twenty minutes, they were almost ready to leave.

At noon, students from a nearby white high school started pouring into Woolworth's. When they first saw us they were sort of surprised. They didn't know how to react. A few started to heckle and the newsmen became interested again. Then the white students started chanting all kinds of anti-Negro slogans. We were called a little bit of everything. The rest of the seats except the three we were occupying had been roped off to prevent others from sitting down. A couple of the boys took one end of the rope and made it into a hangman's noose. Several attempts were made to put it around our necks. The crowds grew as more students and adults came in for lunch.

We kept our eyes straight forward and did not look at the crowd except for occasional glances to see what was going on. All of a sudden I saw a face I remembered — the drunkard from the bus station sit-in. My eyes lingered on him just long enough for us to recognize each other. Today he was drunk, too, so I don't think he remembered where he had seen me before. He took out a knife, opened it, put it in his pocket, and then began to pace the floor. At this point, I told Memphis and Pearlena what was going on. Memphis suggested that we pray. We bowed our heads, and all hell broke loose. A man rushed forward, threw Memphis from his seat, and slapped my face. Then another man who worked in the store threw me against an adjoining counter.

Down on my knees on the floor, I saw Memphis lying near the lunch counter with blood running out of the corners of his mouth. As he tried to protect his face, the man who'd thrown him down kept kicking him against the head. If he had worn hard-soled shoes instead of sneakers, the first kick probably would have killed Memphis. Finally a man dressed in plain clothes identified himself as a police officer and arrested Memphis and his attacker.

Pearlena had been thrown to the floor. She and I got back on our stools after Memphis was arrested. There were some white Tougaloo teachers in the crowd. They asked Pearlena and me if we wanted to leave. They said that things were getting too rough. We didn't know what to do. While we were trying to make up our minds, we were joined by Joan Trumpauer. Now there were three of us and we were integrated. The crowd began to chant, "Communists, Communists, Communists." Some old man in the crowd ordered the students to take us off the stools.

"Which one should I get first?" a big husky boy said.

"That white nigger," the old man said.

The boy lifted Joan from the counter by her waist and carried her out of the store. Simultaneously, I was snatched from my stool by two high school students. I was dragged about thirty feet toward the door by my hair when someone made them turn me loose. As I was getting up off the floor, I saw Joan coming back inside. We started back to the center of the counter to join Pearlena. Lois Chaffee, a white Tougaloo faculty member, was now sitting next to her. So Joan and I just climbed across the rope at the front end of the counter and sat down. There were now four of us, two whites and two Negroes, all women. The mob started smearing us with ketchup, mustard, sugar, pies, and everything on the counter. Soon Joan and I were joined by John Salter, but the moment he sat down he was hit on the jaw with what appeared to be brass knuckles. Blood gushed from his face and someone threw salt into the open wound. Ed King, Tougaloo's chaplain, rushed to him.

At the other end of the counter, Lois and Pearlena were joined by George Raymond, a CORE field worker and a student from Jackson State College. Then a Negro high school boy sat down next to me. The mob took spray paint from the counter and sprayed it on the new demonstrators. The high school student had on a white shirt; the word "nigger" was written on his back with red spray paint.

We sat there for three hours taking a beating when the manager decided to close the store because the mob had begun to go wild with stuff from other counters. He begged and begged everyone to leave. But even after fifteen minutes of begging, no one budged. They would not leave until we did. Then Dr. Beittel, the president of Tougaloo College, came running in. He said he had just heard what was happening.

About ninety policemen were standing outside the store; they had been watching the whole thing through the windows, but had not come in to stop the mob or do anything. President Beittel went outside and asked Captain Ray to come and escort us out. The captain refused, stating the manager had to invite him in before he could enter the premises, so Dr. Beittel himself brought us out. He had told the police that they had better protect us after we were outside the store. When we got outside, the policemen formed a single line that blocked the mob from us. However, they were allowed to throw at us everything they had collected. Within ten minutes, we were picked up by Reverend King in his station wagon and taken to the NAACP headquarters on Lynch Street.

After the sit-in, all I could think of was how sick Mississippi whites were. They believed so much in the segregated Southern way of life, they would kill to preserve it. I sat there in the NAACP office and thought of how many times they had killed when this way of life was threatened. I knew that the killing had just begun. "Many more will die before it is over with," I thought. Before the sit-in, I had always hated the whites in Mississippi. Now I knew it was impossible for me to hate sickness. The whites had a disease, an incurable disease in its final stage. What were our chances against such a disease? I thought of the students, the young Negroes who had just begun to protest, as young interns. When these young interns got older, I thought, they would be the best doctors in the world for social problems.

Before we were taken back to campus, I wanted to get my hair washed. It was stiff with dried mustard, ketchup and sugar. I stopped in at a beauty shop across the street from the NAACP office. I didn't have on any shoes because I had lost them when I was dragged across the floor at Woolworth's. My stockings were sticking to my legs from the mustard that had dried on them. The hairdresser took one look at me and said, "My land, you were in the sit-in, huh?"

"Yes," I answered. "Do you have time to wash my hair and style it?"

"Right away," she said, and she meant right away. There were three other ladies already waiting, but they seemed glad to let me go ahead of them. The hairdresser was real nice. She even took my stockings off and washed my legs while my hair was drying.

There was a mass rally that night at the Pearl Street Church in Jackson, and the place was packed. People were standing two abreast in the aisles. Before the speakers began, all the sit-inners walked out on the stage and were introduced by Medgar Evers. People stood and applauded for what seemed like thirty minutes or more. Medgar told the audience that this was just the beginning of such demonstrations. He asked them to pledge themselves to unite in a massive offensive against segregation in Jackson, and throughout the state. The rally ended with "We Shall Overcome" and sent home hundreds of determined people. It seemed as though Mississippi Negroes were about to get together at last.

Before I demonstrated, I had written Mama. She wrote me back a letter, begging me not to take part in the sit-in. She even sent ten dollars for bus fare to New Orleans. I didn't have one penny, so I kept the money. Mama's letter made me mad. I had to live my life as I saw fit. I had made that decision when I left home. But it hurt to have my family prove to me how scared they were. It hurt me more than anything else — I knew the whites had already started the threats and intimidations. I was the first Negro from my hometown who had openly demonstrated, worked with the NAACP, or anything. When Negroes threatened to do anything in Centreville, they were either shot like Samuel O'Quinn or run out of town, like Reverend Dupree.

I didn't answer Mama's letter. Even if I had written one, she wouldn't have received it before she saw the news on TV or heard it on the radio. I waited to hear from her again. And I waited to hear in the news that someone in Centreville had been murdered. If so, I knew it would be a member of my family.

FOR DISCUSSION

1. Miss Moody describes the bigotry of Southern whites as "an incurable disease in its final stage." Do you think that this is an accurate description?
2. Do you think the objective Miss Moody describes — eating at a lunch counter — is worth the beating she gets and the risks she takes?

James Farmer

(1920–   )

National Director of the Congress of Racial Equality for twenty-four years, James Farmer has devoted much of his life to promoting nonviolence and passive resistance as the means of achieving racial equality in America. Farmer has led Freedom Rides to desegregate Southern bus terminals, and sit-ins in restaurants, theaters, and other public places. Under his leadership, sixty thousand CORE members fought against discrimination in jobs, schools, and housing, investigated cases of police brutality, and organized and encouraged rent strikes in protest of substandard housing conditions. Farmer has also served as a director of the American Civil Liberties Union and as Program Director for the NAACP. The grandson of a slave, Farmer was educated at Wiley College, where his father was a faculty member, and at Howard University School of Divinity. Farmer views education as crucial in the struggle for racial equality. "Black and white students alike," he has observed, "should have the chance to see black men as a proud and equal cultural identity, fitting in with other ethnic entities that go to make up the American pluralistic culture." Farmer is the author of *Freedom—When?* In 1969, he was appointed Assistant Secretary of Health, Education, and Welfare by President Nixon.

A Southern Tale

I would like to begin with the story of an experience I had in the summer of 1963 in Plaquemine, Louisiana. It is, I believe, a tale of the modern South which could be told, with only the details altered, by thousands of civil rights workers in Selma, in Bogalusa, in Meridian. And it can be an instructive introduction to our reflections on the state of freedom in this land.

Until recently Plaquemine was a little town drowsing on the banks of the Mississippi. That difficult balance of social repression with personal benevolence, common to the South, preserved peace and order and a somewhat illusory sense of well-being. The Negroes, at least with one part of their minds, regarded the white people as "good white folks." The whites in turn, with the same part of their minds, thought of the Negroes as jovial and good-natured, content with their lot. They felt honestly surprised when the Negroes began to agitate for the vote.

In the summer of 1963, while many prepared for the famed March on Washington, CORE launched one of its early voter-registration drives in a number of parishes in Louisiana, including Iberville Parish and its principal city of Plaquemine.* Actually there are few Negroes in Plaquemine proper, because the city boundaries have been deliberately engineered to exclude them. The city is horseshoe-shaped, surrounding a Negro community in its midst but refusing to incorporate it legally. As a result this Negro community is deprived of all municipal benefits: the roads are unpaved,

---

*The city of Plaquemine is not to be confused with Plaquemines Parish, the county presided over by the savagely segregationist political boss, Judge Leander Perez.

sewage runs along the streets in open gutters. Understandably a number of people in this utterly disfranchised Negro community showed interest in the registration drive. A few local professional people — the only Negro doctor in the parish, the Negro school principal — at last were coming forward to assume leadership, despite the jeopardy in which such activity placed their jobs.

As a further stimulus to the drive our field secretary from New Orleans, Ronnie Moore, had asked me, in my capacity as National Director (outside agitator number one), to put in an appearance in the area. So I went down to Plaquemine toward the end of August on the first day of what I innocently assumed would be a routine three-day trip. We staged a protest march into town after my speech. When the march was over, all the leaders, myself included, were arrested and taken off to jail in nearby Donaldsonville (which hospitably offered us its facilities in lieu of the already overcrowded Plaquemine jail).

We stayed in jail for a week and a half. As a result, I missed the March on Washington. The timing was unfortunate, but I felt that I really had no choice. Having cast my lot with the people of Plaquemine, I could not simply pull rank and walk out. Moreover, this was my opportunity to reaffirm publicly the insight that CORE had gained during the Freedom Rides of the previous year — that filling the jails could serve as a useful intrument of persuasion. So I sent a message to Washington, which was read by Attorney Floyd B. McKissick, CORE's national chairman, and remained in jail until all the local demonstrators were out. When we came out, the spirit of militancy was spreading in Plaquemine, and two days later a group of young people organized another demonstration, protesting segregation in public places as well as exclusion from the city. This time, however, the marchers did not even get into town. The chief of police stopped them halfway, arrested the leaders, and held the rest of the marchers where they were until state troopers arrived. The troopers came on horseback, riding like cowboys, and they charged into the crowd of boys and girls as if they were rounding up a herd of stampeding cattle. They were armed with billy clubs and cattle prods, which they used mercilessly. Many of the youngsters who fell under the blows were trampled by the horses. (The children of Selma, whose suffering at the hands of police appalled the nation two years later,

were but a part of a spiritual community of brave Southern youngsters like these who for years have been deprived of national
attention by inadequate press coverage.)

This gratuitous savagery inflicted upon their children immediately aroused the adults to a pitch of militancy much more intense
than anything the organizational effort had been able to achieve.
The ministers, who had previously hung back, united for the first
time. (Only one minister, the Rev. Jetson Davis, had been active
in the movement. It was his Plymouth Rock Baptist Church to
which the injured boys and girls had fled for comfort and medical
assistance.) Apathy or fear or whatever had caused their reluctance
dissolved in outrage. The next morning, Sunday, every minister
in the Negro quarter preached a sermon extolling freedom and
condemning police brutality. After church, according to agreement,
they led their congregations to Reverend Davis's church and organized a massive march in protest against the rout of the previous
day. As the time approached for the march to begin, some of
the ministers began to waver. One of them hesitated on his way
to the front of the line. "Where's my wife?" he said, looking around
fearfully. "I don't see my wife. I think I'd better just go on
home." His wife was standing right behind him. "Man," she said,
"if you don't get up there in the front of that line, you ain't got
no wife."

He marched, all right, but his presence could not alter the course
of events. This time when the troopers intercepted the marchers
there was nothing impromptu about the confrontation. They did
not even come on horseback; they came in patrol cars and the horses
arrived in vans. The troopers mounted their horses and assembled
their weapons as if the crowd of unarmed men and women before
them were an opposing army; they charged into the mass as they
had done the day before, flailing with billy clubs and stabbing with
cattle prods. "Get up, nigger!" one would shout, poking a man with
an electric prod and beating him to the ground with a club. "Run,
nigger, run!"

I was waiting at the Plymouth Rock Church. I watched the
Negroes come running back, those who could run, bleeding, hysterical, faint, some of the stronger ones carrying the injured. The
nurse started to bandage the wounds and the rest of us began
to sing "We Shall Overcome"; but the troopers rode roaring

through the streets right up to the door of the church. The Freedom Rock Church, we call it now. They dismounted and broke into the church, yelling and hurling tear gas bombs in front of them — bomb after bomb, poisoning the air. The gas masks protecting the troopers' faces transformed them into monsters as they stood and watched our people growing more and more frantic, screaming with pain and terror, trampling on one another in their frenzied efforts to escape through the back door to the parsonage behind the church. When the people had finally escaped, the troopers set about destroying the empty church. They knocked out the windows, overturned the benches, laid waste everything they could reach, and flooded the gutted building with high-pressure hoses until Bibles and hymnals floated in the aisles.

Then they attacked the parsonage to which we had fled. They sent tear gas bombs smashing through the windows, until all the windows were shattered and almost everyone inside was blinded and choking. The screaming was unbearable. I caught sight of Ronnie Moore administering mouth-to-mouth resuscitation to a young woman. People writhed on the floor, seeking oxygen. A few managed to push through the rear door into the parsonage yard, but the troopers, anticipating them, had ridden around to the back with more bombs to force them in again. And then bombs thrown into the parsonage forced them back out into the yard. All these men and women, who just that morning had resolutely banded together to reach out for freedom and dignity, were reduced now to running from torment to torment, helpless victims of a bitter game.

We tried to telephone for help, but the operators were not putting through any outgoing calls from the Negro section. Within the community, though, there was telephone service, and several calls got through to us in the parsonage. What had appeared to be random and mindless brutality proved to have had a mad purpose after all. It was a manhunt. Troopers were in the streets, kicking open doors, searching every house in the Negro community, overturning chairs and tables, looking under beds and in closets, yelling, "Come on out, Farmer, we know you're in there. Come on out, Farmer! We're going to get you." We could hear the screaming in the streets as the troopers on horseback resumed their sport with the cattle prods and billy clubs: "Get up, nigger! Run, nigger, run!" Holding their victims down with the cattle prod, they were saying, "We'll let you up, nigger, if you tell us where Farmer is." Two of our girls, hiding beneath the church, overhead one trooper saying to another, "When we catch that damn nigger Farmer, we're gonna kill him."

Spiver Gordon, CORE field secretary in Plaquemine, who, people say, looks like me, told me later that he wandered out of the church into the street at this time. Sighting him, state troopers ran up shouting, "Here he is boys. We got Farmer. We got their Jesus." A trooper beckoned to a crowd of hoodlums who were watching nearby, many holding chains, ropes, clubs. "What post we gonna hang him from?" said one. After Spiver convinced them he wasn't me, he took a good lacing for looking like me. An officer said, "He ain't Farmer. You've beat him enough. Put him in the car and arrest him."

There seemed no prospect of aid from any quarter. We were all suffering intensely from the tear gas, and the troopers kept us running with the bombs. In desperation I sent two people creeping through the grass from the parsonage to a funeral hall half a block away to ask for refuge. The owners of the hall agreed to shelter us (although I doubt that they knew what they were taking on). So we crawled on our bellies through the grass, in twos, threes, fours, making use of guerrilla tactics that some remembered from the war but none of us had ever learned as a technique of nonviolent demonstration, until we reached our new sanctuary. Night had fallen by the time all three hundred of us were safely inside, jammed together like straws in a broom into two rooms and a hallway. The sound of screaming still echoed in the streets as the troopers beat down another Negro ("Run, nigger, run!") or invaded another house. The telephones were still useless.

Very shortly the troopers figured out where we were. One of them — a huge, raging, red-faced man — kicked open the back door of the funeral home and screamed, "Come on out, Farmer. We know you're in there. We're gonna get you." I was in the front room. I could look down the hallway, over all the heads, right into his face: it was flushed and dripping with sweat; his hair hung over his eyes, his mouth was twisted. Another trooper burst through the door to stand beside him. "Farmer! Come out!"

I had to give myself up. I felt like a modern Oedipus who, unaware, brought down a plague upon the city. In this hall, their lives endangered by my presence, were three hundred people, many of whom had never even seen me before that day. I began to make my way into the hall, thinking that I would ask to see the warrant for my arrest and demand to know the charges against me. But before I could take three steps the men around me grabbed me silently and pulled me back into the front room, whispering fiercely, "We're not going to let you go out there tonight. That's a lynch mob. You go out there tonight, you won't be alive tomorrow morning."

The trooper, meanwhile, had discovered a large Negro in the back room. He shouted triumphantly: "Here he is, we got that nigger Farmer! Come on in, boys. We got him here."

"I'm not Farmer," he said. A third trooper came in.

"That ain't Farmer," he said. "I know that nigger." They went through his identification papers. He wasn't Farmer.

Suddenly, to everyone's astonishment, a woman pushed her way through the crowd to the back room and confronted the troopers. It was the owner of the funeral home, a "Nervous Nellie," as they say, who had previously held herself apart from the movement. I can never know — she herself probably does not know — what inner revolution or what mysterious force generated in that crowded room plucked her from her caul of fear and thrust her forth to assert with such a dramatic and improbable gesture her new birth of freedom. A funeral hall is as good a place as any for a person to come to life, I suppose, and her action sparked a sympathetic impulse in everyone who watched as she planted herself in front of the first trooper and shook a finger in his face: "Do you have a search warrant to come into my place of business?"

The trooper stared down at her, confounded, and backed away. "No," he said.

"You're not coming into my place of business without a search warrant. I'm a taxpayer and a law-abiding citizen. I have a wake going on here."

I prayed inwardly that her valiant subterfuge would not prove to be a prophecy.

"This ain't no wake," the trooper said, looking around at the throng of angry, frightened people crushed together before him.

"These people ain't at no wake."

"Well, you're not coming into my place of business without a search warrant." The accusing finger pushed him back to the door, where he muttered for a moment to his men outside, then turned and yelled, "All right. We got all the tear gas and all the guns. You ain't got nothin'. We'll give you just five minutes to get Farmer out here. Just five minutes, that's all." He slammed the door.

The door clanged in my ears like the door of a cell in death row. "I'll go out and face them," I said, but once again I was restrained. They would stick by me, these strangers insisted, even if they all had to die, but they would not let me out to be lynched. Someone standing near me pulled out a gun. "Mr. Farmer," he said, "if a trooper comes through that door, he'll be dead."

"If a trooper comes through that door, he may be dead," I conceded. "But what about the trooper behind him and all the ones behind that one? You'll only provoke them into shooting and we won't have a chance." Very reluctantly he allowed me to take the gun from him. It is hard for people to practice nonviolence when they are looking death in the face. I wondered how many others were armed.

Then my own private thoughts engulfed me. Reverend Davis was leading a group in the Lord's Prayer; another group was singing "We Shall Overcome." I was certain I was going to die. What kind of death would it be? Would they mutilate me first? What does it feel like to die? Then I grew panicky about the insurance. Had I paid the last installment? How much was it? I couldn't remember. I couldn't remember anything about it. My wife and little girls — how would it be for them? Abbey was only two then — too young to remember; but Tami was four and a half, and very close to me — she would remember. Well, damn it, if I had to die, at least let the organization wring some use out of my death. I hoped the newspapers were out there. Plenty of them. With plenty of cameras.

I was terrified. The five minutes passed. Six. Seven. Eight. A knock at the front door. My lawyers from New Orleans, Lolis Elie and Robert Collins, identified themselves and squeezed in, breathless. New Orleans radio had broadcast the news that a manhunt was in progress in Plaquemine, and they had driven over immediately. The community, they said, was in a state of siege.

Everywhere one looked one saw troopers, like an invading army. The two lawyers had crawled through the high grass to seek refuge in the graveyard, but when they got there the place came alive: there was a Negro behind every tombstone ("All find safety in the tomb," sang Yeats, in another context). Apparently everyone had counted on the dead to be more hospitable than the living. Apparently, also, everyone knew where I was, but no one was telling the white men. The troopers, it seemed, had been bluffing; they could not be wholly sure I was in the funeral home. It occurred to me that my physical safety, in some elusive way that had very little to do with me, had become a kind of transcendent symbol to all these people of the possibilities of freedom and personal dignity that existed for them. By protecting me, they were preserving their dreams. But did they understand, I wondered, that through their acts of courage during this desperate night they had taken the first great steps toward realizing these possibilities? Did they sense that they had gained at least some of that freedom for which they longed here, and now?

Just as the lawyers finished their story there was another knock at the door. For a moment I thought the troopers had come at last, until I remembered that troopers don't knock. The two men who entered were recently acquired friends from Plaquemine, and pretty rough characters in their own right: my neighbor from town, whom I shall call Fred, and Bill, a buddy of his, ex-Marines who, I knew, carried several guns in their car at all times. The troopers, they told me, had grown systematic. They had set up roadblocks on every street leading out of town. The men who had been waiting in the back had just driven off in the direction of the sheriff's office, presumably to get a search warrant. In short, if I did not get out right now, my life would not be worth a dime.

I told my lawyers to get in their car and try to drive out through the roadblocks. I thought the troopers might respect their identification as attorneys. If they got through, they were to call New York at once, call my wife and tell her I was all right, call Marvin Rich at CORE and have him get in touch with the FBI, call New Orleans and try to get some kind of federal protection. It was imperative that we make contact with the outside world.

Then Fred and Bill set forth their plan. The woman who owned the funeral home had two hearses. They would send the old one out as a decoy with just a driver, who would take it down the main streets, making sure it was spotted at every roadblock. If pursued, he would speed up. Meanwhile, we would try to escape in the second hearse which was waiting, its motor already running, in a garage which we could reach without going out of the house.

If there was something unsettling about the prospect of riding to safety in a hearse, it was nonetheless the logical conclusion to the macabre events of the day. And we could see no alternative. Fred and Bill led the way to the garage, forcing a passage through the sweating men and women who murmured phrases of encouragement and good wishes as we passed. I prayed that our departure would release them from danger, marveling once more at the courage and devotion shown by these strangers.

It was cool, briefly, in the garage, but the hearse was hot and stuffy again. Ronnie Moore, Reverend Davis, and I crawled into the back and crouched down — three restless, nervous men huddled together in a space meant for one motionless body. I thought I remembered that Huey Long had once escaped from someone in a hearse, and for a moment I almost felt like smiling. Someone climbed into the driver's seat and we were off, speeding down the back roads toward New Orleans. Fred and Bill, heavily armed (although I did not know that at the time), followed us in their car. We took a winding route with countless detours over very rough country roads which the Negroes knew more intimately than the whites. Although you can drive from Plaquemine to New Orleans in less than two hours by highway, it took us four and a half hours, despite the fact that we were going very fast and did not stop at all. Whenever a car approached we flattened out on the floor of the hearse until the road was clear again. Our grim destination was another funeral home; our only protection was blackness, a color which had never before promised immunity to Negroes in the South. At times during that wild ride I thought I was already dead. I don't know what the others thought. But when at last we climbed out of the hearse into the hot New Orleans night, we were, by the grace of God and the extraordinary courage of many ordinary men, still very much alive. And not yet entirely out of danger.

When we finally got in touch with the New Orleans CORE, we discovered that our story was already out. The two lawyers had passed the roadblocks and called the authorities in New Orleans, and the press had picked up the news immediately. They had also called my wife, before she had heard anything, to tell her not to worry: "Jim's all right."

"Oh," said Lula. "Why shouldn't he be?"

"There was a little trouble down in Plaquemine, but there's nothing to worry about now. He's out of danger." Whereupon Lula turned on the television set and learned that there was a house-to-house search reportedly going on in Plaquemine, Louisiana, for CORE National Director, James Farmer . . . and, a little later, that James Farmer was reported missing in Plaquemine, Louisiana. She told me later that she turned off the news broadcast and took the children outside where the voices they would hear were less ominous. Shortly afterward, when she went to call the press to try to find out more, she found they were already waiting for her at the house.

In New York, though, they never carried the complete story. The next morning I held a press conference at the CORE headquarters in New Orleans. Newspaper and TV reporters carefully took down all the details, but what they wrote never got farther than New Orleans. But then the list of stories that the newspapers have overlooked in the South and elsewhere is endless.

A trial was scheduled for me the next day in Plaquemine. I was not exactly eager to return but I announced at the press conference that I intended to appear at the appointed time to be served with the warrant for my arrest and to hear the charges, whatever they might be. The FBI sent a man to New York to find out the details from our national office. Our people told him I was going back into Plaquemine the next day and asked if the FBI could guarantee my safety; our attorney, Lolis Elie, called the FBI regional office in New Orleans with the same request. To both requests, the response was the same: the FBI was an investigatory agency, not a protection agency; they could not guarantee my life. However, since the situation was an extraordinary one, they would see what they could do.

With this ambiguous support, Ronnie Moore, Reverend Davis, and I returned somewhat nervously to Plaquemine the next morning. The city police were waiting for us; as soon as we drove into town we saw a policeman in a squad car in front of us announce our arrival into his radio. To our relief FBI agents were everywhere, questioning people in the Negro section, the white section, and around the courthouse. Two agents came over to me as soon as I walked into the courtroom. But as it turned out the troopers had no warrant for my arrest, no charges against me. Nor could we take any action against them, for their name plates and badge numbers had been taped over during the manhunt. In fact, we learned that many of the men who had been riding that night were not even regular troopers: they were ordinary citizens deputized for the occasion.

The drama of Plaquemine ended there, but its consequences are still alive. A new Negro community grew out of that terrible night, aroused, unified, determined to act. When the parish sheriff was up for re-election, the Negro leaders arranged a meeting with his white opponent to ask him about his platform. There was no question of his being an integrationist, of course, but they wanted to know how he stood on the issue of police brutality. Quite emphatically he replied that he was against it, that he had no use for tear gas, billy clubs, or cattle prods, that he had felt that way all his life, and that if he was elected sheriff he would "put a stop to all this nonsense." Just a few days before the election, in a carefully timed maneuver, Reverend Davis, who was also running, withdrew and threw all his votes to this man. He won, too, by a margin so slim there could be no doubt that he owed his victory to the Negro vote. Since assuming office, moreover, he has kept his word on the question of police brutality and has appointed several Negro deputy sheriffs. He is still an uncompromising segregationist: I want to stress that point. Militant nonviolence has not reached his heart, nor is it likely to. But the election of this segregationist sheriff with his policy of decency suggests an important truth which CORE has slowly learned to accept: in the arena of political and social events, what men feel and believe matters much less than what, under various kinds of external pressures, they can be made to *do*. The Negro vote also defeated Jumonville, Iberville's parish state representative and a protégé of Leander Perez, who was alleged by local Negroes to be one of the men deputized to ride that night. Jumonville reportedly accosted one of the Negro leaders after the election with the friendly recommendation that the next time they had a demonstration they had better let him know, because he intended to join them.

But if the hearts of hostile Southerners are likely to be out of reach, the hearts of the men and women involved in the movement are very much within our province. CORE, from its earliest beginnings, has wanted to involve the people themselves, individually, personally, in the struggle for their own freedom. Not simply because it was clear that no one else was going to confer liberty upon them, but because in the very act of working for the impersonal cause of racial freedom, a man experiences, almost like grace, a large measure of private freedom. Or call it a new comprehension of his own identity, an intuition of the expanding boundaries of his self, which, if not the same thing as freedom, is its radical source. This is what happened in Plaquemine to the owner of the funeral home, to the men who kept silence in the graveyard, to the men and women who stood between me and the lynch mob. Gradually, during the course of those two violent days, they made the decision to act instead of being acted upon. The group of people who assembled on Sunday morning were in large part reacting viscerally to the police brutality of the previous day; but the same people that evening, who, although packed together in the funeral hall, refused to be victimized any longer by the troopers, had been transformed into a community of men, capable, despite the severest limitations, of free and even heroic acts. Their subsequent activity at the polls and in initiating a school boycott suggests that this kind of freedom, though essentially personal, will inevitably lead to social action, and that freedom once won is not readily surrendered.

There are also more somber lessons to be drawn from the events at Plaquemine, darker reflections on the future of the movement. CORE is a mass movement now and no longer commands the dedicated allegiance it once did to the principles of nonviolence. What will happen when the Negroes, their self-awareness heightened, experience brutality or repression? What do Negroes and whites really see when they look at each other now that the mists of sleep have been brushed aside? Vision is a terrifying gift. All the energy that has been released is in the service of this vision, and it carries with it a payload of violence.

In the funeral hall in Plaquemine, I overheard two people standing by a window, in a conversation that went something like this:

"Did you see who was ridin' one of those horses? Adams's son!"

"No! You're wrong, they're good white people. Adams has been a friend of our family as long as we've been here. I practically brought his son up."

"Just look at him there, riding one of those horses, with a cattle prod in his hand."

And then a third person said something heard more and more from Negroes in Plaquemine: "The only good white man is a dead one."

The humiliation and fury that a man feels when he has been brutally treated are rendered insupportably bitter if he discovers that he has also been betrayed. You may say that the Negroes will not be susceptible to betrayal much longer, for they are rapidly flinging aside all their illusions about the good will of the white man. But to insure oneself unequivocally against betrayal, one must discard more than illusions; one must also abandon any prospect of trust, or faith, in the white man. And many Negroes are hardening their hearts in this way. They have cast off their outgrown shells, like the mollusks on the beach, and are growing new, more formidable armor which protects them not only from illusion but from conciliation and compromise as well, and in very extreme cases from reason and self-control. On another occasion, I spoke at a rally in West Feliciana Parish which was attended by a number of young Negro men from neighboring Plaquemine. After the meeting I discovered that they all had guns in their cars; they had vowed that nothing was going to happen to Mr. Farmer this time. As we stood outside the church where our meeting had taken place, the sheriff of the parish and a carload of rednecks drove slowly back and forth past the church, then parked on the other side of the street and stared, tauntingly. The young men with me stood with their arms folded, staring back. Tension stretched like a wire across the street. No fight broke out that night, but if it had, the Negroes would have grabbed for their guns. And what will prevent that fight the next time, or the time after that?

Lest you dismiss young boys of this kind as the "hoodlum" element, or the armed ex-Marines in Plaquemine as the "rougher" element, let me make it clear that most Negroes in the South own, or have access to, guns. On the night of the violence in Plaquemine the Negro school principal's mentally retarded son wandered into the street by himself. When his mother realized that he was gone, she became hysterical and grabbed a gun and ran wildly out into the night looking for troopers. Fortunately, someone in her family found her before she found the troopers and dragged her back to the house. But she was ready to shoot. And the seventy-year-old woman at a rally in Canton, Mississippi, who opened her pocketbook to look for something and pulled out a pistol — she was ready to shoot, too. And in Bogalusa, Louisiana, early in 1965, when an already tense racial situation was aggravated by the murder of one of two Negroes on the parish police force — a man who had been hired through the efforts of civil rights workers — the Negroes responded by organizing their own civilian defense force, which they call the Deacons. The Deacons constitute a fully armed and trained militia, holding regular drills, and are prepared to respond with organized violence to any attack upon the Negro community. When I went down to speak in Bogalusa in June, my personal safety was in the hands of the FBI *and* the Deacons.* The CORE people working in Bogalusa have interested the Deacons in a wider program of civil rights, but we haven't persuaded them to give up their arms.

I have often quoted Gandhi to the effect that I would much prefer to see a man resist evil with violence than fail to resist evil out of fear. We grope, of course, for the middle ground, on which evil will be resisted yet violence will be avoided. CORE and the other nonviolent organizations have taken their stand on this middle ground, but the area of their effectiveness seems to be rapidly dwindling. One reason is that the young Negroes are more impatient than the old. Having been less encumbered from the beginning with illusions, they measure progress with a sterner eye. Why should they believe time to be on their side? But another, more difficult reason has to do with the fact that the time it takes for fear to explode into violence is even briefer than the behavior of today's Negroes might indicate. The fear that for so many years bound the Negro to passive acquiescence in his degradation has

* The State Police, the same agency that had sought my blood in Plaquemine, also provided protection.

evaporated. The danger is that in its place a spring of resentment and fury will boil up which can know no expression short of violence.

Luckily the citizens of Plaquemine and Bogalusa, black and white, and the citizens of the rest of the Deep South need not be left to their own devices. However stubbornly these sovereign states may deny it, they are part of one nation, and the resources of this nation — economic, political, moral, and when necessary, military — can and must be used to cure the South of its vicious self-absorption. There are statutes in the U. S. Code forbidding the exclusion of jurors on the grounds of race or color and declaring that jury rolls must be representative of the general population in the areas from which the rolls are drawn. When the federal government enforces these statutes, as it is legally obliged to do, then justice for Negroes in states like Mississippi, Alabama, and Louisiana can become a reality. If the federal government were to withdraw its subsidies from the school lunch programs, the farm programs, the state unemployment services, hospital and highway construction programs, in all cases where these funds are racially administered or serve to promote segregation, then the poorer southern states would be forced to change their ways. After all, the civil rights workers in the South are only doing the job which the federal government ought to be doing for itself: insuring for all citizens the enjoyment of their Constitutional rights.

No one is so ignorant of the South as these Southerners who inveigh against "outside agitators with no understanding of local problems." For they actually suppose that they can restore yesterday *in toto* without soaking their soil in blood. Can they not understand that when we demand "massive federal presence" in the South, we ask not only a show of power to secure our constitutional rights but a reassertion of a just order which we feel alone will preserve the peace for all Southerners? Will they not see that in the example and witness of the black people of the South they are permitted to glimpse the deepest and purest spirit of this nation and that merely by emulating it they can end the moral estrangement which torments them so? We are not only for ourselves.

FOR DISCUSSION

1. Farmer states: "In the arena of political and social events, what men feel and believe matters much less than what, under various kinds of external pressures, they can be made to *do*." Do you agree that actions are more important than attitudes? Do you believe that racial questions can be resolved in spite of the existence of bigotry and hate?
2. Why does Farmer value nonviolence? What does he say are the psychological dangers of violence? Do you think there are corresponding psychological dangers in nonviolence?

New
Directions

John Oliver Killens

(1916–   )

John Oliver Killens, who presently teaches a course in black culture and directs a creative writing workshop at Columbia University, hopes in his writing "to debrainwash" black people about their role in American life. "We have to undo the millions of little white lies that America told itself and the world about the American black man," he has commented. Killens satirizes the black bourgeoisie as well as white hypocrisy; in his latest book, *The Cotillion,* he criticizes black men who have accepted the values imposed by white society. Killens has written several other novels, including *Youngblood, And Then We Heard the Thunder,* and *Sippi.* He is the author of a nonfiction book, *Black Man's Burden;* a play, *Lower Than Angels;* and two screenplays, *Odds Against Tomorrow,* starring Harry Belafonte, and *The Slaves,* starring Ossie Davis and Dionne Warwick. Killens studied at Terrell Law School, Columbia, and New York University. During World War II he served with an amphibious unit in the South Pacific, and before and after the war he served on the National Labor Relations Board. From 1965 to 1968 Killens was writer-in-residence at Fisk University in Nashville, Tennessee.

Negroes Have a Right to Fight Back

There is this scene in the movie *Elmer Gantry*, which was adapted from Sinclair Lewis's novel of the same title, in which this thug is slapping this prostitute around. At which point Burt Lancaster comes in, walks over to the thug and says something like, "Hey, fellow, don't you know that hurts?" And smashes his fist magnificently up against the thug's head and generally kicks the thug around, just to emphasize the point.

It was a beautiful moment in the movie, and it crystallized my own attitude toward the merits (moral and practical) of nonviolence as a policy for Negroes. The perpetrators of violence must be made to know how it feels to be recipients of violence. How can they know unless we teach them?

I remember as a child on Virgin Street in Macon, Georgia, there was this boy who took delight in punching me, and one of his favorite sports was twisting my arm. Onlookers would try to prevail upon him: "Shame! Shame! The Lord is not going to bless you!" Which admonitions seemed to spur my adversary on and on.

One day I put two "alley apples" (pieces of brick) in my trousers' pockets and ventured forth. I was hardly out in the sun-washed

135

streets before Bully-boy playfully accosted me. He immediately began his game of punching me in the stomach, laughing all the while. He was almost a foot taller than I, but I reached into my pockets and leaped up at both sides of his head with the alley apples. Bully-boy ran off. We later became great friends. We never could have become friends on the basis of him kicking my backside, and my counter-attack consisting solely of "Peace, brother!"

The one thing most friends and all enemies of the Afro-American have agreed upon is that we are ordained by nature and by God to be nonviolent. And so a new myth about the Negro is abroad throughout the land, to go with the old myths of laziness and rhythm and irresponsibility and sexual prowess. In the last third of the 20th century, when the disfranchised all over the earth are on the move, the world is being told that the good old U.S.A. has evolved a new type of *Homo sapiens,* the nonviolent Negro. The most disturbing aspect of this question is that many Negroes have bought this myth and are spreading it around.

One of the basic attributes of manhood (when we say manhood, we mean womanhood, selfhood) is the right of self-defense. In the psychological castration of the Negro, the denial of his right of self-defense has been one of the main instruments. Let me make one thing clear: I am not at the moment interested in the question of the so-called castration of the American male by American womanhood, or "Momism." White Mama is a victim too. Indeed, Madame Simone de Beauvoir in *The Second Sex* hit the bull's-eye when she made the analogy between the training of bourgeois girls and the training of American Negroes to know their place and to stay forever in it.

I grew up in Macon under a "separate-but-equal" public-school system. On our way to our wooden-frame school we black kids had to walk through a middle-class white neighborhood. One day in spring a white boy on the way home from his pretty brick school with his comrades said innocently enough, "Hey, nigger, what you learn in school today?" Friendly-like.

"I learned your mother was a pig," the sassy black boy answered, not in the spirit of nonviolence. We were 7 to 11 years of age.

The black boy's buddies laughed angrily, uproariously. The white lad slapped the black boy's face, and that was how the "race riot" started. We fist-fought, we rock-battled, we used sticks and baseball bats and everything else that came to hand. Nobody won. The "race riot" just sort of petered out. We black kids went home with cut lips and bloody noses, but we went home proud and happy and got our backsides whipped for tearing our school clothes, and by the next morning we had almost forgotten it.

Just before noon next day our school ground swarmed with policemen. They strode into the classroom without so much as a "good morning" to the teachers and dragged kids out. They took those who had been in the "riot" and some who'd never even heard of it. The next move was to bring scared black mothers to the jailhouses to whip their children in order to "teach them they must not fight white children." Not a single white lad was arrested — naturally. And so they drove the lesson home. The black American must expect his person to be violated by the white man, but he must know that the white man's person is inviolable.

As an African-American, especially in the hospitable Southland, I concede that nonviolence is a legitimate tactic. It is practical and pragmatic; it has placed the question morally before the nation and the world. But the tendency is to take a tactic and build it into a way of life, to construct a whole new ideology and rhetoric around it. The danger is that all other means of struggle will be proscribed.

We black folk must never, tacitly or otherwise, surrender one single right guaranteed to any other American. The right of self-defense is the most basic of human rights, recognized by all people everywhere. It is certainly more important than the right to eat frankfurters while sitting down, or to get a black haircut in a white barbershop, or to get a night's lodging in Mrs. Murphy's flophouse, may the Good Lord rest her soul. Indeed, it is more important than the right to vote. In many places in the South the Negro can't get to the polls without the right of self-defense.

A man's home is his castle, but a man's "castle" is really made of flesh and bones and heart and soul. One's castle is also one's wife and children, one's people, one's dignity. Invade this castle at your peril is the way the freedom script must read.

I was in Montgomery during the bus-protest movement. I was told on more than one occasion that most Negro men had stopped riding the buses long before the protest started because they could not stand to hear their women insulted by the brave bus drivers. Here the alternatives were sharp and clear: debasement, death, or tired feet. Black citizens of Montgomery did not have the right to be violent, by word or action, toward men who practiced every type of violence against them.

I also know that despite all the preaching about nonviolence, the South is an armed camp. It always has been, ever since I can remember. The first time my wife, who is Brooklyn-born, went south with me, she was shocked to see so many guns in African-American homes. Of course, the white establishment has even vaster fire power, including the guns of the forces of law and order.

Yet, as I said before, nonviolence has the power of moral suasion, which makes it possible to solicit help from many white and liberal summer soldiers, who would otherwise shrink rapidly from the cause. But moral suasion alone never brought about a revolution, for the simple reason that any power structure always constructs for itself a morality which is calculated to perpetuate itself forever. Ask Governor Wallace if the civil rights movement isn't the work of satanic forces. How many centuries of moral suasion would it have taken to convince the kindly Christian Southern slave masters that slavery was evil or to convince the Nazis at Auschwitz that morality was not on their side?

Before leading the Negro people of Birmingham into a demonstration in that city, the Rev. Martin Luther King was reported to have said, "If blood is shed, let it be our blood!" But our blood has always been the blood that was shed. And where is the morality that makes the white racist's blood more sacred than that of black children? I cannot believe that Dr. King meant these words, if indeed he ever uttered them. I can only believe that he got carried away by the dramatics of the moment. Dr. King is one of the men whom I hold in great esteem. We have been friends since 1957. But he loses me and millions of other black Americans when he calls upon us to love our abusers.

"Kick me and I will still love you! Spit on me and I will still love you!"

My daughter, who loves him dearly, heard him say words to this effect on the radio one day. She was in tears for her black hero. "Daddy! Daddy! What's the matter with Rev. King? What's the matter with Rev. King?"

I agree with Chuck and Barbara (my son and daughter). There is no dignity for me in allowing a man to spit on me with impunity. There is only sickness on the part of both of us, and it will beget an ever greater sickness. It degrades me and brutalizes him. If black folk were so sick as to love those who practice genocide against us, we would not deserve human consideration.

The advocates of nonviolence have not reckoned with the psychological needs of black America. There is in many Negroes a deep need to practice violence against their white tormentors. We black folk dearly loved the great Joe Louis, the heavyweight champion the white folk dubbed "The Brown Bomber." Each time he whipped another white man, black hearts overflowed with joy. Joe was strong wine for our much-abused egos.

I was at Yankee Stadium the night our champ knocked out Max Schmeling, the German fighter, in the first round. I saw black men who were strangers embrace each other, unashamedly, and weep for joy. And Joe was in the American tradition. Americans have always been men of violence, and proud of it.

We are a country born in violence. Malcolm X, the Black Nationalist leader who was murdered, knew this basic truth. He did not preach violence, but he did advocate self-defense. That is one of the reasons he had such tremendous attraction for the people of the ghetto. What I am saying is that the so-called race riots are healthier (from the point of view of the ghetto people) than the internecine gang warfare which was the vogue in the ghettos a few years ago, when black teen-agers killed each other or killed equally helpless Puerto Ricans, as was often the case in New York City. Historically in the black ghettos the helpless and hopeless have practiced violence on each other. Stand around the emergency entrance at Harlem Hospital of a Saturday night and check the business in black blood drawn by black hands that comes in every weekend.

It is time for Americans (black and white) to stop hoodwinking themselves. Nonviolence is a tactic, but it must never be a way of life for the black American. Just because I love myself, the black *Me*, why do white Americans (especially liberals) think it means I have to hate the white American *You?* We black and white folk in the U.S.A. have to settle many things between us before the matter of love can be discussed. For one thing, if you practice violence against me, I mean to give it back to you in kind.

Most black folk believe in the kind of nonviolence that keeps everybody nonviolent. For example: In a certain cotton county in the heart of Dixieland, black folk, most of them sharecroppers, asserted their right to vote and were driven from the land. For several years they lived in tents, and of a Saturday evening white pranksters had a playful way of driving out to Tent City and shooting into it. A couple of campers were injured, including a pregnant woman. Complaints to the authorities got no results at all. So one Saturday evening when the pranksters turned up, just to have a little sport, the campers (lacking a sense of humor) returned the fire. A young relative of the sheriff got his arm shattered. The sheriff got out there in a hurry and found rifles shining out of every tent. He sent for the Negro leader.

"Tell them to give up them rifles, boy. I can't protect 'em less'n they surrender up them rifles."

Whereupon the 35-year-old "boy" said, "We figured you was kind of busy, Sheriff. We thought we'd give you a helping hand and protect our own selves." There was no more racial violence in the county for a long time.

Let us speak plainly to each other. Your black brother is spoiling for a fight in affirmation of his selfhood. This is the meaning of Watts and Harlem and Bedford-Stuyvesant. It seems to me, you folk who abhor violence, you are barking up the wrong tree when you come to black folk and call on them to be nonviolent. Go to the attackers. Go to the ones who start the fire, not to the firefighters. Insist that your Government place the same premium on black life as it does on white. As far as I can ascertain, no white American has ever been condemned to death by the courts for taking a black life.

The Deacons of Defense, the Negro self-defense organization that started in Louisiana not long ago, is going to mushroom and increasingly become a necessary appendage to the civil rights movement. This should be welcomed by everyone who is sincere about the "Negro revolution." It accomplishes three things simultaneously. It makes certain that the Government will play the role of the fire department, the pacifier. Second: The actual physical presence of the Deacons (or any similar group) will go a long way in staying the hands of the violence makers. Third: It further affirms the black Americans' determination to exercise every right enjoyed by all other Americans.

Otherwise we're in for longer and hotter summers. There are all kinds among us black folks. Gentle ones and angry ones, forgiving and vindictive, and every single one is determined to be free. Julian Bond, poet, SNCC leader, and duly elected member of the Georgia legislature (his seat was denied him because of his pronouncements on Vietnam), summed up the situation when he wrote:

> Look at that gal shake that thing.
> We cannot all be Martin Luther King.

I believe he meant, among other things, that whites cannot expect Negroes to be different — that is, more saintly than whites are — and that most black folk are in no mood to give up the right to defend themselves.

FOR DISCUSSION

1. At what times and under what conditions does Killens think that violence is necessary and morally acceptable? Do you agree?
2. Killens says that "One of the basic attributes of manhood. . . is the right of self-defense." What does Killens mean by the word "manhood"? What is your own definition of the word? Is self-defense a necessary part of manhood? Why or why not?
3. Killens asks: "How many centuries of moral suasion would it have taken to convince the kindly Christian Southern slave masters that slavery was evil?" What does Killens mean by "moral suasion"? Do you think that moral suasion can ever overcome evil?
4. Killens says that "Americans have always been men of violence and proud of it." Drawing on your experience and reading, do you agree with this statement?

Julius Lester

(1939–   )

The author of *To Be a Slave, Folktales,* and *Look Out, Whitey! Black Powers's Gon' Get Your Mama,* a history of the Black Power movement, Lester is interested in black culture and in human rights, as is evident from his many political activities. He served as field secretary for the Student Nonviolent Coordinating Committee, attended the Bertrand Russell War Crimes Tribunal in Stockholm, and traveled to Vietnam to photograph the bombing there. He has conducted his own radio program, "The Great Proletarian Cultural Revolution" and has taught "The History of Black Resistance" at the New School for Social Research. He has written poetry, books for children, and articles for *Village Voice, New York Free Press,* and *Broadside.* Two albums of his songs have been recorded, and he has also co-authored with Pete Seeger a book entitled *The Twelve String Guitar as Played by Leadbelly.*

Black Pawns in a White Game

AXIOM: White folks do nothing that is not to their advantage.

CORRECTION: White folks do nothing that they *think* is not to their advantage.

CONCLUSION: White folks do nothing that is not to the disadvantage of blacks.

SOLUTION: Every time the white man comes to help you, check out his motive and what he's getting out of it. Once you know, figure out how you can get what you want without him getting what he wants. Don't forget: America owes you everything. You've paid your dues. You owe America nothing.

One of the bigger lies that America has given the world is that Lincoln freed the slaves, and that blacks should be grateful from can to can't because Mr. Lincoln was so generous. It is true that Lincoln affixed his signature to a proclamation giving the slaves their freedom and that the slaves, thereby, were free to "get hat." It is not true that Lincoln did so out of the goodness of his heart or that we have to be grateful to him. What does it matter why he did it? Isn't it sufficient that he did it? No, because white folks

143

never miss an opportunity to tell us "what we did for you people." ("Why, I gave five dollars and a box of hominy grits to CORE last year.") The black schoolchild grows up feeling half-guilty for even thinking about cussing out a white man, because he's been taught that it was a white man who gave us freedom. How many times has the photograph been reprinted of the small Negro boy staring up at the huge statue of Lincoln at the Lincoln Memorial? The photograph would mean nothing if the boy doing the staring were white. What is the catechism the black child learns from Grade One on? "Class, what did Abraham Lincoln do?" "Lincoln freed the slaves," and the point is driven home that you'd still be down on Mr. Charlie's plantation working from can to can't if Mr. Lincoln hadn't done your great-great-grandmama a favor. (Every black person in America can trace his ancestry back to Africa by way of a bill of sale. It's easier to trace the history of a piece of furniture than the family history of a black person.)

Blacks have no reason to feel grateful to Abraham Lincoln. Rather, they should be angry at him. After all, he came into office in 1861. How come it took him two whole years to free the slaves? His pen was sitting on his desk the whole time. All he had to do was get up one morning and say, "Doggonit! I think I'm gon' free the slaves today. It just ain't right for folks to own other folks." It was that simple. Mr. Lincoln, however, like Mr. Kennedy (take your pick) and Mr. Eastland, moved politically, not morally. He said that if he could keep the Union together by maintaining slavery, he'd do it. If he had to free the slaves to keep the Union together, he'd do that, too. But he was in office to preserve the Union, not free the slaves. (Nowadays they say preserve law and order, not see that blacks get a little justice.)

The Civil War is represented in school textbooks as a war to free the slaves. It turned out that way, but that ain't the way it started out. (Let's be serious. White folks ain't gon' engage in four years of bloody fighting over the condition of niggers. We're supposed to believe that nonsense, though.)

At the beginning of the War the Union army was under strict orders not to interfere with slavery. When one general seized two counties in Virginia, he immediately issued a proclamation to this effect to the local white people. Another Union officer "returned" two black men whom he caught heading north. Now, it's uncertain whether the two were slaves or freedmen, but that never entered the officer's mind. They were black and if they weren't previously slaves, they were after they ran into him. On July 4, 1861, Colonel Pryor of Ohio went so far as to deliver a speech to the people of Virginia, saying, "I desire to assure you that the relation of master and servant as recognized in your state shall be respected. Your authority over that species of property shall not in the least be interfered with. To this end, I assure you that those under my command have peremptory orders to take up and hold any Negroes found running about the camp without passes from their masters."

At the beginning of the war the Reluctant Emancipator, Lincoln, had the Secretary of State inform all foreign governments that the war was not one of abolition. Frederick Douglass analyzed the situation well. The Civil War was begun "in the interests of slavery on both sides. The South was fighting to take slavery out of the Union and the North was fighting to keep it in the Union; the South fighting to get it beyond the limits of the United States Constitution, and the North fighting for the old guarantees — both despising the Negro, both insulting the Negro."

But Mr. Lincoln hadn't reckoned on US. Everywhere the Union army set foot, we showed up with our wives, children, aunts, uncles, grandparents, and anybody else who'd come. The situation that General Butler faced at Fortress Monroe in Virginia was typical: "On May twenty-sixth, only two days after the one slave appeared before Butler, eight Negroes appeared; on the next day, forty-seven of all ages and both sexes. Each day they continued to come by twenties, thirties and forties until by July 30th the number had reached nine hundred. In a very short while the number ran up into the thousands. The renowned Fortress took the name of the 'freedom fort' to which the blacks came by means of a 'mysterious spiritual telegraph.'"

The Committee of the American Freedmen's Union Commission gave an even more graphic description. "Imagine, if you will, a slave population . . . coming garbed in rags or in silks, with feet shod or bleeding, individually or in families and larger groups — an army of slaves and fugitives. . . . The arrival among us of these hordes was like the oncoming of cities. . . ."

Generally history books mention the coming of the slaves to

the Union lines as (1) a problem for the troops, who had thousands of illiterate, dirty niggers trailing after them; or (2) an example of the Union's benevolence in accepting them. Both miss the point. By coming to Union lines, the blacks had, in effect, gone on strike. Slave labor was essential to the success of the Confederate army, because the rebels didn't eat if the blacks didn't stay at home and grow the food. DuBois says, "It was a general strike that involved directly in the end perhaps a half million people."

There were other factors operating which finally made Lincoln and the Union army take a pragmatic approach to blacks. With the general strike against the plantations by a half-million slaves, there still remained some three million on the plantations. Lincoln saw clearly that by freeing these he could cripple the South. Too, the Union was having a difficult time recruiting whites to fight the war. A popular poem of the period summed up the feelings of most whites. It was called "Sambo's Right to Be Kilt."

> *Some say it is a burnin' shame*
> *To make the naygurs fight,*
> *An' that the thrade of bein' kilt*
> *Belongs but to the white;*

> *But as for me upon my sowl'*
> *So liberal are we here,*
> *I'll let Sambo be murthered in place o' meself*
> *On every day in the year.*

So strong was the feeling of whites against the war that there were antidraft riots in many Northern cities. Black leaders, like Douglass, were vehement in their agitation that black men be allowed to fight in the war. Lincoln finally saw that the war could not be won otherwise. The other operative factor was that England was preparing to recognize the South as a separate nation and was building iron-clad warships for the Confederacy. This could be stopped only by an order proclaiming the slaves free. English public sentiment was so vehement against slavery that an emancipation proclamation would create intense pro-Union feeling and deter the English government from interfering. The Emancipation Proclamation was staring Mr. Lincoln dead in the eye.

W. E. B. DuBois pointed out: "The North started out with the idea of fighting the war without touching slavery. They faced the fact, after severe fighting, that Negroes seemed a valuable asset as laborers, and they therefore declared them 'contraband of war' [property belonging to the enemy and valuable to the invader]. It was but a step from that to attract and induce black labor to help the Northern armies. Slaves were urged and invited into the Northern armies; they became military laborers and spies; not simply military laborers, but laborers on the plantations, where the crops went to help the Federal army or were sold North. Thus where Northern armies appeared, Negro laborers came, and the North found itself actually freeing slaves before it had the slightest intention of doing so, indeed when it had every intention not to."

During the period from 1830 to the end of the Civil War, black men exercised a power out of proportion to their numbers. Today, however, whites tell us that we have little choice but to temper our demands, because we are only ten percent of the population. This is a reflection of the typical American regard for quantity and size. These whites choose to forget that ten percent of the U.S. population controls ninety percent of the wealth and that the United States itself has only six percent of the world's population and dominates half the world (and is trying mighty hard to dominate the other half). As a black I am not impressed with any view that says I am a minority that must accede to the will of the majority. From 1830 to 1860 blacks were *less* than ten percent of the population, yet they played a decisive role. Those who say that they were sitting on the porch pining for ol' massa to come home or off in the woods drinking rotgut and singing the blues are mistaken. Whatever was done to free the slaves, blacks were in the vanguard. They were not freed because of the moral conscience of the government. They were freed because the government was forced to free them. They did not accomplish the task alone. The Abolitionists exerted a certain pressure on the government. The antidraft riots, the need for the North to industrialize, exerted another kind of pressure. There were many factors which led to the Emancipation Proclamation, and it is not only misleading, but a lie, to depict Lincoln as the Great Emancipator.

Once the slaves were free and the war over, everybody had the same question: what shall we do with the Negro? Lincoln had an interesting proposal. Send them back to Africa. (Most of them had been born in America; so he meant, send them to Africa.)

He had advanced the idea in 1862, while trying to get black leaders to support his plan then of sending blacks to New Granada in Central America. "Your race suffer greatly, many of them, by living among us, while ours suffer from your presence. In a word we suffer on each side. If this is admitted, it affords a reason why we should be separated. If not for the institution of slavery and the colored race as a basis, the war could not have an existence."

Frederick Douglass told him where it was at. "A horse thief pleading that the existence of the horse is the apology for his theft or a highway man contending that the money in the traveller's pocket is the sole first cause of his robbery are about as much entitled to respect as is the President's reasoning at this point. No, Mr. President, it is not the innocent horse that makes the horse thief, nor the traveller's purse that makes the highway robber, and it is not the presence of the Negro that causes this foul and unnatural war, but the cruel and brutal cupidity of those who wish to possess horses, money and Negroes by means of theft, robbery, and rebellion."

Some blacks wanted to and did go to Africa after the war, founding the Republic of Liberia. The rest stayed, while the white folks wondered what to do with them. Frederick Douglass once again responded with his accustomed eloquence: ". . . do nothing! . . . Your *doing* with Negroes is their greatest misfortune. . . . The Negro should have been let alone in Africa . . . let alone when the pirates and robbers offered him for sale in our Christian slave markets . . . let alone by the courts, judges, politicians, legislators and slave drivers. . . . If you see him plowing in the open field, levelling the forest, at work with a spade, a rake, a hoe, a pick-axe, or a bill — let him alone; he has a right to work. If you see him, on his way to school with spelling book, geography and arithmetic in his hands — let him alone; . . . If he has a ballot in his hand and is on his way to the ballot-box . . . let him *alone*. . . ."

They couldn't let him alone, though. It was not to their advantage. The emphasis of Reconstruction was on the reconstruction of the South and the country was in no mood to draw up new architectural plans to include blacks. The North had already done something it really hadn't intended to — freed the slaves. Having been forced that far, it would be forced no further.

The Abolitionists abandoned the struggle after emancipation, feeling that the victory was won. (The struggle only begins when *la guerre est finie*.) Douglass argued passionately that a victory was not a victory until it was ensured, and he could see signs that it would not be. First, the vote had to be procured for blacks. Even here there was opposition. Foner points out that, "Women who had been active Abolitionists now argued that before the 'ignorant black men' should be given the ballot, intelligent and cultured white women should be enfranchised. Some ardent feminists went as far as to appeal to the Southerners to support their cause on the ground that the enfranchisement of women would provide a bulwark in the South against Negro rule."

Douglass and other black leaders felt that only with the vote would freedom be ensured. Charles Sumner, the Massachusetts senator, was a strong advocate of this view. The vote was eventually procured through the fight put up in Congress by the so-called Radical Republicans. Getting the vote, however, was not enough. Blacks needed what a congressman from Pennsylvania, Thaddeus Stevens, fought for in Congress — forty acres and a mule. Blacks could not be really free until they had economic independence. If they could not work for themselves, they had to work for someone else. In the South, the someone else could only be those who had held them slaves. Nominally free they would be, but the economic power would remain where it was. To have the vote was essential, but it was not enough.

Reconstruction not only rebuilt the South, it reconstructed the nation. The white folks had fought each other for four years, and Reconstruction saw them getting back together. In the North, the war had done the one thing it was designed to do: it had made business prosper. The steel industry was created by the needs of the war, and the basis for modern industry was laid. Suddenly the coal, iron, oil, forests, and other natural resources of the West became important to the North and the North was anxious to get out there and get them. The resources could be used, though, only if the railroad was developed into a nationwide transportation system. All this could be done if business was able to consolidate its political power before the former slaveholding Southerners reentered Congress. To do this, business and the Republican party, which were almost synonymous, had to come out in support of black suffrage. It could not align itself with the western states, because they were angry over the high taxes the Republicans were levying to pay off the costs of the war; and when the South reentered Congress, the West would align itself with the South. The Republican party could not have withstood such a coalition. Therefore, the Republican party got the vote, aligning itself temporarily with the liberal elements of the North; it made a coalition with democratic forces. (A decided contradiction in terms, because it is impossible for capitalism to be truly democratic, but if it is in the interest of business, it will feign democratic principles as long as they are profitable.)

The status of man in America has always been one of a commodity. Something to be bought and sold, fought over and discussed in terms of his usefulness to others in gaining their ends. The commodity status of whites has always been disguised and made palatable; the commodity status of blacks has never been disguised, and instead of its being made palatable, it has been rammed down the throat without even the afterthought of a glass of water to ease the pain.

Blacks were the pawns in Reconstruction as they had been during the war. DuBois has pointed out that "If Northern industry before the war had secured a monopoly of the raw material raised in the South for its new manufactures; and if Northern and Western labor could have maintained their wage scale against slave competition, the North would not have touched the slave system. But this the South had frustrated. It had threatened labor with nationwide slave competition and had sent its cotton abroad to buy cheap manufactures, and had resisted the protective tariff demanded by the North." Thus, the war was inevitable, "because the South was determined to make free white labor compete with black slaves, monopolize land and raw material in the hands of a political aristocracy, and extend the scope of that power; war, because the industrial North refused to surrender its raw material and one of its chief markets to Europe; war, because white American labor, while it refused to recognize black labor as equal and human, had to fight to maintain its own humanity and ideal of equality."

The labor movement never saw that its own best interest lay in supporting not only emancipation and suffrage, but land redistribution also. Economic independence for the black meant economic independence for the white. Business saw to it that the whites never realized this. It was easy to play upon the prejudice and fears already extant. When Northern and Western labor began to organize against the high taxes of the Republicans, business was more than aware that the end result of such organization would be economic independence for the worker. It was relatively simple to point a finger at the black man as being the source of the problem, to sacrifice the black man for a coalition with the old landed aristocracy of the South. The ex-Confederates would return to power as they desired, and Northern money, having consolidated its business interests, was free to expand into the South as well as the West. No longer needing blacks, business easily sacrificed them with the Compromise of 1876.

The loser was not only the black man, but all American labor. As William Sylvis, president of the International Labor Movement, put it in the late nineteenth century: ". . . when the shackles fell from the limbs of those four millions of blacks, it did not make them *free* men; it simply transferred them from one condition of slavery to another; it placed them upon the platform of the white working man, and made all slaves together. I do not mean that freeing the Negro enslaved the white; I mean that we were slaves before; always have been, and that the abolition of the right of property in man added four millions of black slaves to the white slaves of the country. We are now all one family of slaves together, and the labor reform movement is a second emancipation proclamation."

There was a second emancipation proclamation and it was business that was emancipated. Labor refused to have blacks in most unions. Taking advantage of this, business used racist arguments to hide its own exploitation of whites.

FOR DISCUSSION

1. According to Lester, what caused Lincoln to free the slaves?
2. What does Lester mean by the title of this essay? What does he say that black people wanted and needed after the Civil War? Does Lester believe that black people are really better off today?
3. In this selection, Lester often uses a humorous tone in discussing serious issues. Give examples of this technique and explain why you think the technique is or is not effective.

LeRoi Jones

(1934–   )

LeRoi Jones has written, "Any man, black or white, has something to say, but a black man these days will seem to have something more profound to say." The message which Jones conveys in his writing comes across to his audience with raw power and explosive violence. *Dutchman,* his first professionally produced play, won him the 1964 off-Broadway Obie Award, and productions of *The Slave, The Toilet, The Eighth Ditch,* and *The Baptism* have also called attention to his forceful artistic talent. Jones views himself primarily as a poet, however. *Preface to a Twenty Volume Suicide Note,* published in 1961, typifies his difficult poetic form. Jones has also written numerous social essays, printed in *Negro Digest* and *Evergreen Review,* has edited Greenwich Village publications, and has written articles on jazz for *Downbeat* and *Jazz Review.* Often as well known for his involvement in social and political affairs as for his writing, Jones was arrested in 1964 for possession of firearms. His case received particular attention when the judge quoted one of Jones's militant poems in court before sentencing him to a term in prison. The conviction was later reversed. Jones attended Rutgers and graduated from Howard; later he received his M.A. in German literature from Columbia, where he has since lectured. Jones's literary contributions have been described as a form of "cultural nationalism" and as an attempt to enhance purpose and esteem in black communications.

Tokenism: 300 Years
for Five Cents

In Marietta, Georgia, the Lockheed Airplane people maintain a plant that employs more than 10,000 people, only a few of whom are black people. As is customary in the South, all the black people who work in that Lockheed plant work at menial jobs such as porters, messengers, haulers, etc. Recently, however, the national office of the NAACP and the Federal Government have been chiding the Lockheed people to hire Negroes in capacities other than the traditional porter-messenger syndrome. And I suppose it is a credit to those organizations that they finally did get Lockheed to concur with their wishes; in fact, the Marietta plant promoted one of their Negro porters to a clerical position. This move was hailed by the Federal Government, the NAACP, and similar secret societies as "a huge step forward in race relations" (to quote from *The New York Times*). The Negro who received the promotion, thus becoming "a symbol of American determination to rid itself of the stigma of racial discrimination" (*op. cit.*), was shown smiling broadly (without his broom) and looking generally symbolic. *The Times* added that this promotion and this symbolic move toward "racial understanding" also gives the ex-porter a five-cents-an-hour increase, or two dollars more a week. This means that instead of forty-five dollars a week (if, indeed, the porter made that much) this blazing symbol of social progress now makes forty-seven dollars a week.

There are almost 20,000,000 Negroes in the United States. One of these 20 million has been given a two-dollar raise and promoted to a clerical job that my two-year-old daughter could probably work out without too much trouble. And we are told that this act

153

is *symbolic* of the "gigantic strides the Negro has taken since slavery."

In 1954, the Supreme Court ruled that segregated schools were illegal, and that, indeed, segregation in public schools should be wiped out "with all deliberate speed." Since 1954, this ruling has affected about 6.9 per cent of the nearly 4,000,000 Negro students in Southern segregated schools, and there are four states, Mississippi, South Carolina, Georgia, and Alabama, who have ignored the ruling entirely. And yet, here again, we are asked to accept the ruling itself (with its hypocritical double-talk — what is "all deliberate speed"?) as yet another example of "the gigantic strides," etc. The fact that the ruling affects only 6.9 per cent of 4,000,000 Negro students in the South (and this percentage stands greatly boosted by the inclusion of figures from the "liberal" border states such as Maryland, Missouri, and the District of Columbia — in fact Maryland and the District account for *more than half* of the total percentage) apparently does not matter to the liberals and other eager humanists who claim huge victories in their "ceaseless war on inequality."

Negroes have been in this country since the early part of the seventeenth century. And they have only "legally" been free human beings since the middle of the nineteenth. So we have two hundred years of complete slavery and now for the last one hundred years a "legal" freedom that has so many ands, ifs, or buts that I, for one, cannot accept it as freedom at all but see it as a legal fiction that has been perpetuated to assuage the occasional loud rumbles of moral conscience that must at times smite all American white men.

These last hundred years, according to our official social chiropractors, have been for American Negroes years of progress and advancement. As *Time* magazine said, "Never has the Negro been able to purchase so much and never has he owned so much, free and clear." That is, everything but his own soul. It is not "progress" that the majority of Negroes want, but Freedom. And I apologize if that word, Freedom, sounds a little too unsophisticated or a little too much like 1930's social renaissance for some people; the fact remains that it is the one thing that has been most consistently denied the Negro in America (as well as black men all over the world).

Self-determination is the term used when referring to some would-be nation's desire for freedom. The right to choose one's own path. The right to become exactly what one thinks himself capable of. And it strikes me as monstrous that a nation or, for that matter, a civilization like our Western civilization, reared for the last five hundred years exclusively in the humanistic bombast of the Renaissance, should find it almost impossible to understand the strivings of enslaved peoples to free themselves. It is this kind of paradox that has caused the word "Nationalism" to be despised and/or feared in the West, or shrugged off in official circles as "just another Communist plot." Even here in the United States the relatively mild attempts at "integration" in the South are met by accusations of being Communist-inspired. (And I would add as, say, a note of warning to the various Southern congressmen whose sole qualification for office is that they are more vociferous in their disparagement of Negroes than their opponents, that if they persist in crediting the Communists with every attempt at delivering the black American out of his real and constant bondage, someone's going to believe them . . . namely the new or aspirant nations of Asia, Latin America, and Africa.)

2

Actual slavery in the United States was supposed to have been brought to an end by the Civil War. There is rather bitter insistence in the point that it was *Americans* who were supposedly being freed; the African slaves had long since become American slaves. But it is by now almost a truism to point out that there was much more at stake in that war than the emancipation of the slaves. The Civil War, or at least the result of the Civil War, was undoubtedly the triumph of the Northern industrial classes over the Southern agricultural classes. As so many writers have termed it, "the triumph of American capitalism." The small oligarchy of American industrial capital had overcome its last great enemy, the rich Southern planter, and was now more or less free to bring the very processes of American government under its control.

But on the surface the Civil War looked like a great moral struggle out of which the side of right and justice had emerged victorious. The emancipation of Negroes, the passage, by the

Republican Congress, of the 13th, 14th and 15th amendments (to give a "legal basis" for black citizenship), and the setting up of the Reconstruction governments in the South, all gave promise that a new era had arrived for Negroes. And in fact it had, but was of a complexion which was not immediately apparent, and was certainly not the new era most Negroes would have looked forward to.

The Reconstruction governments fell because the Northern industrialists joined with the planter classes of the South to disfranchise the Negro once again, frightened that a "coalition" of the poor and disfranchised Southern whites — the agrarian interests — and the newly freed Negroes might prove too strong a threat to their designs of absolute political and economic control of the South. As E. Franklin Frazier points out in *Black Bourgeoisie*, "When agrarian unrest among the 'poor whites' of the South joined forces with the Populist movement, which represented the general unrest among American farmers, the question of race was used to defeat the co-operation of 'poor whites' and Negroes. It was then that the demagogues assumed leadership of the 'poor whites' and provided a solution of the class conflict among whites that offered no challenge to the political power and economic privileges of the industrialists and the planter class. The program, which made the Negro the scapegoat, contained the following provisions: (1) The Negro was completely disfranchised by all sorts of legal subterfuges, with the threat of force in the background; (2) the funds which were appropriated on a per capita basis for Negro school children were diverted to white schools; and (3) a legal system of segregation in all phases of public life was instituted. In order to justify this program, the demagogues, who were supported by the white propertied classes, engaged for twenty-five years in a campaign to prove that the Negro was subhuman, morally de-generate and intellectually incapable of being educated."

3

Tokenism, or what I define as the setting up of social stalemates or the extension of meager privilege to some few "selected" Negroes in order that a semblance of compromise or "progress," or a lessening in racial repression might seem to be achieved, while actually helping to maintain the status quo just as rigidly, could not, or course, really come into being until after the emancipation. Before that, there was no real need to extend even a few tokens to the slave. There was, indeed, no reason why anyone had to create the illusion for the slave that he was "making progress," or governing himself, or any other such untruth. In a sense, however, the extension of "special privileges" to Negro house servants ("house niggers") did early help to create a new *class* of Negro, within the slave system. The "house nigger" not only assimilated "massa's" ideas and attitudes at a rapid rate, but his children were sometimes allowed to learn trades and become artisans and craftsmen. And it was these artisans and craftsmen who made up the bulk of the 500,000 black "freedmen" extant at the beginning of the Civil War.

The Reconstruction governments are the first actual example of the kind of crumb-dropping that was to characterize the Federal Government's attitude regarding the status of the "free" Negro. The Reconstruction governments were nothing but symbols, since no real lands were ever given to the Negroes, and even any political influence which had come to the ex-slaves as part of the Reconstruction was nullified by 1876 (the so-called redemption of the South).

Another aspect of tokenism is the setting apart or appointing of "leaders" among Negroes who in effect glorify whatever petty symbol the white ruling classes think is necessary for Negroes to have at that particular time. So, at the fall of the Reconstruction governments, the industrialist-financier-planter oligarchy found an able "leader" in Booker T. Washington, a Negro through whom these interests could make their wishes known to the great masses of Negroes. After the North had more or less washed its hands of the whole "Southern mess," and it was a generally accepted idea that the Negroes had ruined the Reconstruction simply because they were incapable of governing themselves, Booker T. Washington came into great prominence and influence as a Negro leader because he accepted the idea of segregation as a "solution" to the race problem, and also because he advocated that Negroes learn trades rather than go into any of the more ambitious professions.

"Coming from Booker T. Washington, who enjoyed entré into the society of Standard Oil executives, railroad magnates, and

Andrew Carnegie, the strategy was persuasive. Washington avowed his loyalty to laissez faire, took his stand in the South as a Southerner, and accepted social inequality for the forseeable future. Blocked by the power of the whites and told by their own spokesman that 'white leadership is preferable,' most Negroes followed . . ." (from *The Contours Of American History*, W. A. Williams).

The wealth and influence of the great industrialists backed the Washington solution and as Williams points out, "Washington's position was made almost impregnable through the generosity of Northern white philanthropists who liked his ideology (which included a code of labor quietism and even strikebreaking)." Negro intellectuals like W. E. B. DuBois who attacked Washington's position had little chance to shake it, opposed by such formidable opponents as the monied interests and the philanthropists, who replaced the "radical republican" idea of actually redistributing land to the freed Negroes with ineffective philanthropies such as Howard University or Tuskegee (which was Booker T.'s pet — a college for Negroes that taught trades, *e.g.*, carpentry, masonry). And of course, as it was intended, the tokens did very little to improve the general conditions of Negroes anywhere. The Sumner-Stevens plan of redistributing land among the freedmen, in fact even breaking up the large plantations and making small farms for both white and black would have changed the entire history of this country had it been implemented in good faith. But such an idea definitely proved a threat to the hold of the planters and industrialists over the politics and economy of the South. So it was defeated.

4

Radicals like DuBois (who left Atlanta University so he would not embarrass them wih his opinions) helped set up the National Association for the Advancement of Colored People in 1909. At that time the organization was considered extremely radical, and it was merely asking — but for the first time — for "complete equality." Most of the financiers and philanthropists who made a sometime hobby out of extending stale crumbs to Negroes denounced the organization. Also, most of the so-called Negro middle class could not abide by the radicalism of the organization's program, and some of them (the Negro educators in particular, who depended on the philanthropists for their bread, butter, and prestige) brought as much pressure as they could on the fledgling NAACP to modify its policies. (And I think it is not too violent a digression to ask just what kind of men or what kind of desperation would have to be inflicted upon a man's soul in order for him to say that giving him equal rights in his own country is "too radical"? E. Franklin Frazier does a very good job in *Black Bourgeoisie* of describing the type of man who would be capable of such social pathology.) But radicalism or no, when the First World War ended and the great exodus of Negroes from the South began, membership in the NAACP grew tremendously. Yet despite the great support the NAACP received from the Negro masses in its incunabula, the organization was more and more influenced by its white liberal supporters and gradually modified its program and position to that of the white middle class, thereby swiftly limiting its appeal to the middle-class Negro. Today, the NAACP is almost completely out of touch with the great masses of blacks and bases its programs on a "liberal" middle-class line, which affects only a very tiny portion of the 20,000,000 Negroes living in the United States. It has, in fact, become little more than a token itself.

5

A rich man told me recently that a liberal is a man who tells other people what to do with their money. I told him that that was right from the side of the telescope he looked through, but that as far as I was concerned a liberal was a man who told other people what to do with their poverty.

I mention this peculiarly American phenomenon, *i.e.,* American Liberalism, because it is just this group of amateur social theorists, American Liberals, who have done most throughout American history to insure the success of tokenism. Whoever has proposed whatever particular social evasion or dilution — to whatever ignominious end — it is usually the liberal who gives that lie the greatest lip service. They, liberals, are people with extremely heavy consciences and almost nonexistent courage. Too little is always enough. And it is always the *symbol* that appeals to them most. The single futile housing project in the jungle of slums and disease eases the liberals' conscience, so they are loudest in praising it —

even though it might not solve any problems at all. The single black student in the Southern university, the promoted porter in Marietta, Georgia — all ease the liberals' conscience like a benevolent but highly addictive drug. And, for them, "moderation" is a kind of religious catch phrase that they are wont to mumble on street corners even alone late at night.

Is it an excess for a man to ask to be free? To declare, even vehemently, that no man has the right to dictate the life of another man? Is it so radical and untoward for nations to claim the right of self-determination? Freedom *now!* has become the cry of a great many American Negroes and colonial nations. Not freedom "when you get ready to give it," as some spurious privilege or shabby act of charity; but *now!* The liberal says, "You are a radical." So be it.

Liberals, as good post-Renaissance men, believe wholeheartedly in *progress.* There are even those people who speak knowingly about "progress in the arts." But progress is not, and never has been the question as far as the enslaving of men is concerned. Africans never asked to be escorted to the New World. They never had any idea that learning "good English" and wearing shoes had anything to do with the validity of their lives on earth. Slavery was not anything but an unnecessarily cruel and repressive method of making money for the Western white man. Colonialism was a more subtle, but equally repressive method of accomplishing the same end. The liberal is in a strange position because his conscience, unlike the conscience of his richer or less intelligent brothers, has always bothered him about these acts, but never sufficiently to move him to any concrete action except the setting up of palliatives and symbols to remind him of his own good faith. In fact, even though the slave trade, for instance, was entered into for purely commercial reasons, after a few years the more liberal-minded Americans began to try to justify it as a method of converting heathens to Christianity. And, again, you can see how perfect Christianity was for the slave then; a great number of slave uprisings were dictated by the African's gods or the new slaves' desire to return to the land of their gods. As I put it in a recent essay on the sociological development of blues: "You can see how necessary, how perfect, it was that Christianity came first, that the African was given something 'to take his mind off Africa,' that he was forced, if he still wished to escape the filthy paternalism and cruelty of slavery, to wait at least until he died, when he could be transported peacefully and majestically to 'the promised land.'" I'm certain the first Negro spirituals must have soothed a lot of consciences as well as enabling a little more relaxation among the overseers. It almost tempts me toward another essay tentatively titled *Christianity as a Deterrent to Slave Uprisings.* More tokens.

A Negro who is told that the "desegregation" of a bus terminal in Georgia somehow represents "progress" is definitely being lied to. Progress to where? The bare minimum of intelligent life is what any man wants. This was true in 1600 when the first slaves were hauled off the boats, and it has not changed. Perhaps the trappings and the external manifestations that time and the lessons of history have proposed make some things seem different or changed in the world, but the basic necessities of useful life are the same. If a tractor has replaced a mule, the need to have the field produce has not changed. And if a black man can speak English now, or read a newspaper, whereas (ask any liberal) he could not in 18 so-and-so, he is no better off now than he was then if he still cannot receive the basic privileges of manhood. In fact, he is perhaps worse off than in 18 so-and-so since he is now being constantly persuaded that he *is* receiving these basic privileges (or, at least, he is told that he soon will, *e.g.,* R. Kennedy's high comic avowal that perhaps in forty years a Negro might be President).

But, for me, the idea of "progress" is a huge fallacy. An absurd Western egoism that has been foisted on the rest of the world as an excuse for slavery and colonialism. An excuse for making money. Because this progress the Western slavemaster is always talking about means simply the mass acquisition of all the dubious fruits of the industrial revolution. And the acquisition of material wealth has, in my mind, only very slightly to do with self-determination or freedom. Somehow, and most especially in the United States, the fact that more Negroes can buy new Fords this year than they could in 1931 is supposed to represent some great stride *forward.* To where? How many Fords will Negroes have to own before police in Mississippi stop using police dogs on them? How many television sets and refrigerators will these same Negroes have to own before they are allowed to vote without being made to live in tents, or their children allowed decent educations? And even if a bus station in Anniston, Alabama, is "integrated," how much does this help reduce the 25 per cent unemployment figure that besets Negroes in Harlem.

If, right this minute, I were, in some strange fit of irrationality, to declare that "I am a free man and have the right of complete self-determination," chances are that I would be dead or in jail by nightfall. But being an American Negro, I am supposed to be conditioned to certain "unfortunate" aspects of American democracy. And all my reactions are supposedly based on this conditioning, which is, in effect, that even as a native born American, etc., etc., there are certain things I cannot do because I have a black skin. Tokenism is that philosophy (of psychological exploitation) which is supposed to assuage my natural inclinations toward complete freedom. For the middle-class Negro this assuagement can take the form it takes in the mainstream of American life, *i.e.*, material acquisition, or the elevating of one "select" coon to some position that seems heaped in "prestige," *e.g.*, Special Delegate to the United Nations, Director of Public Housing, Assistant Press Secretary to the President of the United States, Vice President In Charge of Personnel for Chock Full O' Nuts, Borough President of Manhattan, etc. The "Speaking Of People" column in *Ebony* magazine is the banal chronicler of such "advances," *e.g.*, the first Negro sheriff of Banwood, Utah, or the first Negro Asst. Film Editor for BRRR films. But the lower class Negro cannot use this kind of tokenism, so he is pretty much left in the lurch. But so effective is this kind of crumb-dropping among the *soi-disant* black middle class that these people become the actual tokens themselves, or worse. Thus when an issue like the treacherous relief cuts in Newburgh, New York, presents itself, the black middle class is actually likely to side with reactionaries, even though, as in the Newburgh case, such a situation harms a great many poorer Negroes. This kind of process reaches perhaps its most absurd, albeit horrible, manifestation when a man like George Schuyler, in the Negro paper *The Pittsburgh Courier,* can write editorials *defending the Portuguese* in Angola, even after the United States Government itself had been pressured into censuring this NATO ally. It is also a man like Schuyler who is willing to support one of the great aphorisms of tokenism (this one begun by the worst elements of racist neo-colonialism) that somehow a man, usually a black man, must "make progress to freedom." That somehow, a man must show he is *"ready* for independence or self-determination." A man is either free or he is not. There cannot be any apprenticeship for freedom. My God, what makes a black man, in America or Africa, or any of the other oppressed colonial peoples of the world, less ready for freedom than the average *Daily News* reading American white man?

But again, while it is true that there is a gulf of tokens seemingly separating the middle-class Negro from the great masses of Negroes (just as there is seemingly a great gulf of tokens separating the "select cadre" of a great many colonial countries from their oppressed people), I insist that it is only an artificial separation, and that the black bourgeoisie (and their foreign cousins) are no better off than the poorest Negro in this country. But how to tell the *first* Negro Asst. Film Editor of BRRR films that he is just as bad off as the poorest and most oppressed of his black brothers? Tokenism is no abstract philosophy; it was put into action by hardheaded realists.

But realists or no, there is in the world now among most of its oppressed peoples, a growing disaffection with meaningless platitudes, and a reluctance to be had by the same shallow phrases that have characterized the hypocritical attitude of the West toward the plight of the American black man and all colonial peoples. There will be fewer and fewer tragedies like the murder of Patrice Lumumba. The new nations will no longer allow themselves to be sucked in by these same hackneyed sirens of tokenism or malevolent liberalism. The world, my friends, is definitely changing.

FOR DISCUSSION

1. Jones defines "liberals" as "people with extremely heavy consciences and almost nonexistent courage." What does he mean? How do you think a man of genuine courage should live and act if he believes that all men are entitled to equal freedom and justice?
2. Jones says that tokenism preserves the status quo. Explain what tokenism means and give examples of it. Drawing upon your own experience, explain how Jones's statement is or is not true.

Eldridge Cleaver
(*1935–*   )

Eldridge Cleaver, who describes himself as "a full time revolutionary in the struggle for black liberation in America," is best known for his association with the Black Panther Party, an organization whose purpose is to protect black people. Born in Little Rock, Arkansas, in 1935, Cleaver grew up in the black ghetto of Los Angeles. While serving a prison sentence, he began writing essays which were later published as the best-seller *Soul on Ice*.

After his release from prison, Cleaver assumed the position of Minister of Information for the Black Panther Party. One of their most effective spokesmen, he began writing articles for *Ramparts, Esquire,* and other magazines. He also spoke at the University of California at Berkeley. In 1968, he was nominated for President by the Peace and Freedom Party. Earlier that year he was arrested for participating in a gun battle with police in Oakland, California. Rather than return to prison, Cleaver fled the country.

The White Race
and Its Heroes

White people cannot, in the generality, be taken as models of how to live. Rather, the white man is himself in sore need of new standards, which will release him from his confusion and place him once again in fruitful communion with the depths of his own being.

James Baldwin
The Fire Next Time

Right from the go, let me make one thing absolutely clear: I am not now, nor have I ever been, a white man. Nor, I hasten to add, am I now a Black Muslim — although I used to be. But I *am* an Ofay Watcher, a member of that unchartered, amorphous league which has members on all continents and the islands of the seas. Ofay Watchers Anonymous, we might be called, because we exist concealed in the shadows wherever colored people have known oppression by whites, by white enslavers, colonizers, imperialists, and neo-colonialists.

Did it irritate you, compatriot, for me to string those epithets out like that? Tolerate me. My intention was not necessarily to sprinkle salt over anyone's wounds. I did it primarily to relieve a certain pressure on my brain. Do you cop that? If not, then we're in trouble, because we Ofay Watchers have a pronounced tendency to slip

165

into that mood. If it is bothersome to you, it is quite a task for me because not too long ago it was my way of life to preach, as ardently as I could, that the white race is a race of devils, created by their maker to do evil, and make evil appear as good; that the white race is the natural, unchangeable enemy of the black man, who is the original man, owner, maker, cream of the planet Earth; that the white race was soon to be destroyed by Allah, and that the black man would then inherit the earth, which has always, in fact, been his.

I have, so to speak, washed my hands in the blood of the martyr, Malcolm X, whose retreat from the precipice of madness created new room for others to turn about in, and I am now caught up in that tiny space, attempting a maneuver of my own. Having renounced the teachings of Elijah Muhammad, I find that a rebirth does not follow automatically, of its own accord, that a void is left in one's vision, and this void seeks constantly to obliterate itself by pulling one back to one's former outlook. I have tried a tentative compromise by adopting a select vocabulary, so that now when I see the whites of *their* eyes, instead of saying "devil" or "beast" I say "imperialist" or "colonialist," and everyone seems to be happier.

In silence, we have spent our years watching the ofays, trying to understand them, on the principle that you have a better chance coping with the known than with the unknown. Some of us have been, and some still are, interested in learning whether it is *ultimately* possible to live in the same territory with people who seem so disagreeable to live with; still others want to get as far away from ofays as possible. What we share in common is the desire to break the ofays' power over us.

At times of fundamental social change, such as the era in which we live, it is easy to be deceived by the onrush of events, beguiled by the craving for social stability into mistaking transitory phenomena for enduring reality. The strength and permanence of "white backlash" in America is just such an illusion. However much this rear-guard action might seem to grow in strength, the initiative, and the future, rest with those whites and blacks who have liberated themselves from the master/slave syndrome. And these are to be found mainly among the youth.

Over the past twelve years there has surfaced a political conflict between the generations that is deeper, even, than the struggle between the races. Its first dramatic manifestation was within the ranks of the Negro people, when college students in the South, fed up with Uncle Tom's hat-in-hand approach to revolution, threw off the yoke of the NAACP. When these students initiated the first sit-ins, their spirit spread like a raging fire across the nation, and the technique of nonviolent direct action, constantly refined and honed into a sharp cutting tool, swiftly matured. The older Negro "leaders," who are now all die-hard advocates of this tactic, scolded the students for sitting-in. The students rained down contempt upon their hoary heads. In the pre-sit-in days, these conservative leaders had always succeeded in putting down insurgent elements among the Negro people. (A measure of their power, prior to the students' rebellion, is shown by their success in isolating such great black men as the late W. E. B. DuBois and Paul Robeson, when these stalwarts, refusing to bite their tongues, lost favor with the U.S. Government by their unstinting efforts to link up the Negro revolution with national liberation movements around the world.)

The "Negro leaders," and the whites who depended upon them to control their people, were outraged by the impudence of the students. Calling for a moratorium on student initiative, they were greeted instead by an encore of sit-ins, and retired to their ivory towers to contemplate the new phenomenon. Others, less prudent because held on a tighter leash by the whites, had their careers brought to an abrupt end because they thought they could lead a black/white backlash against the students, only to find themselves in a kind of Bay of Pigs. Negro college presidents, who expelled students from all-Negro colleges in an attempt to quash the demonstrations, ended up losing their jobs; the victorious students would no longer allow them to preside over the campuses. The spontaneous protests on Southern campuses over the repressive measures of their college administrations were an earnest of the Free Speech upheaval which years later was to shake the UC campus at Berkeley. In countless ways, the rebellion of the black students served as catalyst for the brewing revolt of the whites.

What has suddenly happened is that the white race has lost its heroes. Worse, its heroes have been revealed as villains and its greatest heroes as the arch-villains. The new generations of whites, appalled by the sanguine and despicable record carved over the face of the globe by their race in the last five hundred years, are rejecting the panoply of white heroes, whose heroism consisted in erecting the inglorious edifice of colonialism and imperialism; heroes whose careers rested on a system of foreign and domestic exploitation, rooted in the myth of white supremacy and the manifest destiny of the white race. The emerging shape of a new world order, and the requisites for survival in such a world, are fostering in young whites a new outlook. They recoil in shame from the spectacle of cowboys and pioneers — their heroic forefathers whose exploits filled earlier generations with pride — galloping across a movie screen shooting down Indians like Coke bottles. Even Winston Churchill, who is looked upon by older whites as perhaps the greatest hero of the twentieth century — even he, because of the system of which he was a creature and which he served, is an arch-villain in the eyes of the young white rebels.

At the close of World War Two, national liberation movements in the colonized world picked up new momentum and audacity, seeking to cash in on the democratic promises made by the Allies during the war. The Atlantic Charter, signed by President Roosevelt and Prime Minister Churchill in 1941, affirming "the right of all people to choose the form of government under which they may live," established the principle, although it took years of postwar struggle to give this piece of rhetoric even the appearance of reality. And just as world revolution has prompted the oppressed to re-evaluate their self-image in terms of the changing conditions, to slough off the servile attitudes inculcated by long years of subordination, the same dynamics of change have prompted the white people of the world to re-evaluate their self-image as well, to disabuse themselves of the Master Race psychology developed over centuries of imperial hegemony.

It is among the white youth of the world that the greatest change is taking place. It is they who are experiencing the great psychic pain of waking into consciousness to find their inherited heroes turned by events into villains. Communication and understanding between the older and younger generations of whites has entered a crisis. The elders, who, in the tradition of privileged classes or races, genuinely do not understand the youth, trapped by old ways of thinking and blind to the future, have only just begun to be vexed — because the youth have only just begun to rebel. So thoroughgoing is the revolution in the psyches of white youth that the traditional tolerance which every older generation has found it necessary to display is quickly exhausted, leaving a gulf of fear, hostility, mutual misunderstanding, and contempt.

The rebellion of the oppressed peoples of the world, along with the Negro revolution in America, have opened the way to a new evaluation of history, a re-examination of the role played by the white race since the beginning of European expansion. The positive achievements are also there in the record, and future generations will applaud them. But there can be no applause now, not while the master still holds the whip in his hand! Not even the master's own children can find it possible to applaud him — he cannot even applaud himself! The negative rings too loudly. Slave-catchers, slaveowners, murderers, butchers, invaders, oppressors — the white heroes have acquired new names. The great white statesmen whom school children are taught to revere are revealed as the architects of systems of human exploitation and slavery. Religious leaders are exposed as condoners and justifiers of all these evil deeds. Schoolteachers and college professors are seen as a clique of brainwashers and whitewashers.

The white youth of today are coming to see, intuitively, that to escape the onus of the history their fathers made they must face and admit the moral truth concerning the works of their fathers. That such venerated figures as George Washington and Thomas Jefferson owned hundreds of black slaves, that all of the Presidents up to Lincoln presided over a slave state, and that every President since Lincoln connived politically and cynically with the issues affecting the human rights and general welfare of the broad masses of the American people — these facts weigh heavily upon the hearts of these young people.

The elders do not like to give these youngsters credit for being able to understand what is going on and what has gone on. When speaking of juvenile delinquency, or the rebellious attitude of today's youth, the elders employ a glib rhetoric. They speak of the "alienation of youth," the desire of the young to be independent, the problems of "the father image" and "the mother image" and their effect upon growing children who lack sound models upon which to pattern themselves. But they consider it bad form to connect the problems of the youth with the central event of our era — the national liberation movements abroad and the Negro revolution at home. The foundations of authority have been blasted to bits in America because the whole society has been indicted, tried, and convicted of injustice. To the youth, the elders are Ugly Americans; to the elders, the youth have gone mad.

The rebellion of the white youth has gone through four broadly discernible stages. First there was an initial recoiling away, a rejection of the conformity which America expected, and had always received, sooner or later, from its youth. The disaffected youth were refusing to participate in the system, having discovered that America, far from helping the underdog, was up to its ears in the mud trying to hold the dog down. Because of the publicity and self-advertisements of the more vocal rebels, this period has come to be known as the beatnik era, although not all of the youth affected by these changes thought of themselves as beatniks. The howl of the beatniks and their scathing, outraged denunciation of the system — characterized by Ginsberg as Moloch, a bloodthirsty Semitic deity to which the ancient tribes sacrificed their firstborn children — was a serious, irrevocable declaration of war. It is revealing that the elders looked upon the beatniks as mere obscene misfits who were too lazy to take baths and too stingy to buy a haircut. The elders had eyes but couldn't see, ears but couldn't hear — not even when the message came through as clearly as in this remarkable passage from Jack Kerouac's *On the Road:*

> At lilac evening I walked with every muscle aching among the lights of 27th and Welton in the Denver colored section, wishing I were a Negro, feeling that the best the white world had offered was not enough ecstasy for me, not enough life, joy, kicks, darkness, music, not enough night. I wished I were a Denver Mexican, or even a poor overworked Jap, anything but what I so drearily was, a "white man" disillusioned. All my life I'd had white ambitions. . . . I passed the dark porches of Mexican and Negro homes; soft voices were there, occasionally the dusky knee of some mysterious sensuous gal; the dark faces of the men behind rose arbors. Little children sat like sages in ancient rocking chairs.

The second stage arrived when these young people, having decided emphatically that the world, and particularly the U.S.A., was unacceptable to them in its present form, began an active search for roles they could play in changing the society. If many of these young people were content to lay up in their cool beat pads, smoking pot and listening to jazz in a perpetual orgy of esoteric bliss, there were others, less crushed by the system, who recognized the need for positive action. Moloch could not ask for anything more than to have its disaffected victims withdraw into safe, passive, apolitical little nonparticipatory islands, in an economy less and less able to provide jobs for the growing pool of unemployed. If all the unemployed had followed the lead of the beatniks, Moloch would gladly have legalized the use of euphoric drugs and marijuana, passed out free jazz albums and sleeping bags, to all those willing to sign affidavits promising to remain "beat." The non-beat disenchanted white youth were attracted magnetically to the Negro revolution, which had begun to take on a mass, insurrectionary tone. But they had difficulty understanding their relationship to the Negro, and what role "whites" could play in a "Negro revolution." For the time being they watched the Negro activists from afar.

The third stage, which is rapidly drawing to a close, emerged when white youth started joining Negro demonstrations in large numbers. The presence of whites among the demonstrators emboldened the Negro leaders and allowed them to use tactics they never would have been able to employ with all-black troops. The racist conscience of America is such that murder does not register as murder, really, unless the victim is white. And it was only when the newspapers and magazines started carrying pictures and stories of white demonstrators being beaten and maimed by mobs and police that the public began to protest. Negroes have become so used to this double standard that they, too, react differently to the death of a white. When white freedom riders were brutalized along with blacks, a sigh of relief went up from the black masses, because the blacks knew that white blood is the coin of freedom in a land where for four hundred years black blood has been shed unremarked and with impunity. America has never truly been outraged by the murder of a black man, woman, or child. White politicians may, if Negroes are aroused by a particular murder, say with their lips what they know with their minds they should feel with their hearts — but don't.

It is a measure of what the Negro feels that when the two white and one black civil rights workers were murdered in Mississippi in 1964, the event was welcomed by Negroes on a level of understanding beyond and deeper than the grief they felt for the victims and their families. This welcoming of violence and death to whites can almost be heard — indeed it can be heard — in the inevitable words, oft repeated by Negroes, that those whites, and blacks, do not die in vain. So it was with Mrs. Viola Liuzzo. And much of the anger which Negroes felt toward Martin Luther King during the Battle of Selma stemmed from the fact that he denied history a great moment, never to be recaptured, when he turned tail on the Edmund Pettus Bridge and refused to all those whites behind him what they had traveled thousands of miles to receive. If the police had turned them back by force, all those nuns, priests, rabbis, preachers, and distinguished ladies and gentlemen old and young — as they had done the Negroes a week earlier — the violence and brutality of the system would have been ruthlessly exposed. Or if, seeing King determined to lead them on to Montgomery, the troopers had stepped aside to avoid precisely the confrontation that Washington would not have tolerated, it would have signaled the capitulation of the militant white South. As it turned out, the March on Montgomery was a show of somewhat dim luster, stage-managed by the Establishment. But by this time the young whites were already active participants in the Negro revolution. In fact they had begun to transform it into something broader, with the potential of encompassing the whole of America in a radical reordering of society.

The fourth stage, now in its infancy, sees these white youth taking the initiative, using techniques learned in the Negro struggle to attack problems in the general society. The classic example of this new energy in action was the student battle on the UC campus at Berkeley, California — the Free Speech Movement. Leading the revolt were veterans of the civil rights movement, some of whom spent time on the firing line in the wilderness of Mississippi/Alabama. Flowing from the same momentum were student demonstrations against U.S. interference in the internal affairs of Vietnam, Cuba, the Dominican Republic, and the Congo and U.S. aid to apartheid in South Africa. The students even aroused the intellectual community to actions and positions unthinkable a few years ago: witness the teach-ins. But their revolt is deeper than single-issue protest. The characteristics of the white rebels which most alarm their elders — the long hair, the new dances, their love for Negro music, their use of marijuana, their mystical attitude toward sex — are all tools of their rebellion. They have turned these tools against the totalitarian fabric of American society — and they mean to change it.

From the beginning, America has been a schizophrenic nation. Its two conflicting images of itself were never reconciled, because never before has the survival of its most cherished myths made a reconciliation mandatory. Once before, during the bitter struggle between North and South climaxed by the Civil War, the two images of America came into conflict, although whites North and South scarcely understood it. The image of America held by its most alienated citizens was advanced neither by the North nor by the South; it was perhaps best expressed by Frederick Douglass, who was born into slavery in 1817, escaped to the North, and became the greatest leader-spokesman for the blacks of his era. In words that can still, years later, arouse an audience of black Americans, Frederick Douglass delivered, in 1852, a scorching indictment in his Fourth of July oration in Rochester:

> What to the American slave is your Fourth of July? I answer: a day that reveals to him, more than all other days in the year, the gross injustice and cruelty to which he is the constant victim. To him your celebration is a sham; your boasted liberty, an unholy licence; your national greatness, swelling vanity; your sounds of rejoicing are empty and heartless; your denunciation of tyrants, brass-fronted impudence; your shouts of liberty and equality, hollow mockery; your prayers and hymns, your sermons and thanksgivings, with all your religious parade and solemnity, are, to him, more bombast, fraud, deception, impiety and hypocrisy — a thin veil to cover up crimes which would disgrace a nation of savages. . . .
>
> You boast of your love of liberty, your superior civilization, and your pure Christianity, while the whole political power of the nation (as embodied in the two great political parties) is

solemnly pledged to support and perpetuate the enslavement
of three millions of your countrymen. You hurl your anathemas
at the crown-headed tyrants of Russia and Austria and pride
yourselves on your democratic institutions, while you yourselves consent to be the mere *tools* and *bodyguards* of the tyrants
of Virginia and Carolina.

You invite to your shores fugitives of oppression from
abroad, honor them with banquets, greet them with ovations,
cheer them, toast them, salute them, protect them, and pour
out your money to them like water; but the fugitive from your
own land you advertise, hunt, arrest, shoot, and kill. You glory
in your refinement and your universal education; yet you maintain a system as barbarous and dreadful as ever stained the
character of a nation — a system begun in avarice, supported
in pride, and perpetuated in cruelty.

You shed tears over fallen Hungary, and make the sad story
of her wrongs the theme of your poets, statesmen, and orators,
till your gallant sons are ready to fly to arms to vindicate her
cause against the oppressor; but, in regard to the ten thousand
wrongs of the American slave, you would enforce the strictest
silence, and would hail him as an enemy of the nation who
dares to make these wrongs the subject of public discourse!

This most alienated view of America was preached by the Abolitionists, and by Harriet Beecher Stowe in her *Uncle Tom's Cabin.*
But such a view of America was too distasteful to receive wide
attention, and serious debate about America's image and her reality
was engaged in only on the fringes of society. Even when confronted with overwhelming evidence to the contrary, most white
Americans have found it possible, after steadying their rattled
nerves, to settle comfortably back into their vaunted belief that
America is dedicated to the proposition that all men are created
equal and endowed by their Creator with certain inalienable
rights — life, liberty and the pursuit of happiness. With the Constitution for a rudder and the Declaration of Independence as its

guiding star, the ship of state is sailing always toward a brighter vision of freedom and justice for all.

Because there is no common ground between these two contradictory images of America, they had to be kept apart. But the moment the blacks were let into the white world — let out of the voiceless and faceless cages of their ghettos, singing, walking, talking, dancing, writing, and orating *their* image of America and of Americans — the white world was suddenly challenged to match its practice to its preachments. And this is why those whites who abandon the *white* image of America and adopt the *black* are greeted with such unmitigated hostility by their elders.

For all these years whites have been taught to believe in the myth they preached, while Negroes have had to face the bitter reality of what America practiced. But without the lies and distortions, white Americans would not have been able to do the things they have done. When whites are forced to look honestly upon the objective proof of their deeds, the cement of mendacity holding white society together swiftly disintegrates. On the other hand, the core of the black world's vision remains intact, and in fact begins to expand and spread into the psychological territory vacated by the non-viable white lies, *i.e.,* into the minds of young whites. It is remarkable how the system worked for so many years, how the majority of whites remained effectively unaware of any contradiction between their view of the world and that world itself. The mechanism by which this was rendered possible requires examination at this point.

Let us recall that the white man, in order to justify slavery and, later on, to justify segregation, elaborated a complex, all-pervasive myth which at one time classified the black man as a subhuman beast of burden. The myth was progressively modified, gradually elevating the blacks on the scale of evolution, following their slowly changing status, until the plateau of separate-but-equal was reached at the close of the nineteenth century. During slavery, the black was seen as a mindless Supermasculine Menial. Forced to do the backbreaking work, he was conceived in terms of his ability to do such work — "field niggers," etc. The white man administered the plantation, doing all the thinking, exercising omnipotent power over the slaves. He had little difficulty dissociating himself from the black slaves, and he could not conceive of their positions being reversed or even reversible.

Blacks and whites being conceived as mutually exclusive types, those attributes imputed to the blacks could not also be imputed to the whites — at least not in equal degree — without blurring the line separating the races. These images were based upon the social function of the two races, the work they performed. The ideal white man was one who knew how to use his head, who knew how to manage and control things and get things done. Those whites who were not in a position to perform these functions nevertheless aspired to them. The ideal black man was one who did exactly as he was told, and did it efficiently and cheerfully. "Slaves," said Frederick Douglass, "are generally expected to sing as well as to work." As the black man's position and function became more varied, the images of white and black, having become stereotypes, lagged behind.

The separate-but-equal doctrine was promulgated by the Supreme Court in 1896. It had the same purpose domestically as the Open Door Policy toward China in the international arena: to stabilize a situation and subordinate a non-white population so that racist exploiters could manipulate those people according to their own selfish interests. These doctrines were foisted off as *the epitome of enlightened justice, the highest expression of morality.* Sanctified by religion, justified by philosophy and legalized by the Supreme Court, separate-but-equal was enforced by day by agencies of the law, and by the KKK & Co. under cover of night. Booker T. Washington, the Martin Luther King of his day, accepted separate-but-equal in the name of all Negroes. W. E. B. DuBois denounced it.

Separate-but-equal marked the last stage of the white man's flight into cultural neurosis, and the beginning of the black man's frantic striving to assert his humanity and equalize his position with the white. Blacks ventured into all fields of endeavor to which they could gain entrance. Their goal was to present in all fields a performance that would equal or surpass that of the whites. It was long axiomatic among blacks that a black had to be twice as competent as a white in any field in order to win grudging recognition from the whites. This produced a pathological motivation in blacks to equal or surpass the whites, and a pathological motivation in the whites to maintain a distance from the blacks. This is the rack on which black and white Americans receive their delicious torture! At first there was the color bar, flatly denying the blacks entrance to certain spheres of activity. When this no longer worked, and blacks invaded sector after sector of American life and economy, the whites evolved other methods of keeping their distance. The illusion of the Negro's inferior nature had to be maintained.

One device evolved by the whites was to tab whatever the blacks did with the prefix "Negro." We had *Negro* literature, *Negro* athletes, *Negro* music, *Negro* doctors, *Negro* politicians, *Negro* workers. The malignant ingeniousness of this device is that although it accurately describes an objective biological fact — or, at least, a sociological fact in America — it concealed the paramount psychological fact: that to the white mind, prefixing anything with "Negro" automatically consigned it to an inferior category. A well-known example of the white necessity to deny due credit to blacks is in the realm of music. White musicians were famous for going to Harlem and other Negro cultural centers literally to steal the black man's music, carrying it back across the color line into the Great White World and passing off the watered-down loot as their own original creations. Blacks, meanwhile were ridiculed as *Negro* musicians playing inferior coon music.

The Negro revolution at home and national liberation movements abroad have unceremoniously shattered the world of fantasy in which the whites have been living. It is painful that many do not yet see that their fantasy world has been rendered uninhabitable in the last half of the twentieth century. But it is away from this world that the white youth of today are turning. The "paper tiger" hero, James Bond, offering the whites a triumphant image of themselves, is saying what many whites want desperately to hear reaffirmed: *I am still the White Man, lord of the land, licensed to kill, and the world is still an empire at my feet.* James Bond feeds on that secret little anxiety, the psychological white backlash, felt in some degree by most whites alive. It is exasperating to see little brown men and little yellow men from the mysterious Orient, and the opaque black men of Africa (to say nothing of these impudent American Negroes!) who come to the UN and talk smart to us, who are scurrying all over *our* globe in their strange modes of dress — much as if they were new, unpleasant arrivals from another planet. Many whites believe in their ulcers that it is only a matter of time before the Marines get the signal to round up these truants and put them back securely in their cages. But it is away from this fantasy world that the white youth of today are turning.

In the world revolution now under way, the initiative rests with people of color. That growing numbers of white youth are repudiating their heritage of blood and taking people of color as their heroes and models is a tribute not only to their insight but to the resilience of the human spirit. For today the heroes of the initiative are people not usually thought of as white: Fidel Castro, Che Guevara, Kwame Nkrumah, Mao Tse-tung, Gamal Abdel Nasser, Robert F. Williams, Malcolm X, Ben Bella, John Lewis, Martin Luther King, Jr., Robert Parris Moses, Ho Chi Minh, Stokely Carmichael, W. E. B. DuBois, James Forman, Chou En-lai.

The white youth of today have begun to react to the fact that the "American Way of Life" is a fossil of history. What do they care if their old baldheaded and crew-cut elders don't dig their caveman mops? They couldn't care less about the old honkies who don't like their new dances: Frug, Monkey, Jerk, Swim, Watusi. All they know is that it feels good to swing to way-out body-rhythms instead of dragging across the dance floor like zombies to the dead beat of mind-smothered Mickey Mouse music. Is it any wonder that the youth have lost all respect for their elders, for law and order, when for as long as they can remember all they've witnessed is a monumental bickering over the Negro's place in American society and the right of people around the world to be left alone by outside powers? They have witnessed the law, both domestic and international, being spat upon by those who do not like its terms. Is it any wonder, then, that they feel justified, by sitting-in and freedom riding, in breaking laws made by lawless men? Old funny-styled, zipper-mouthed political night riders know nothing but to haul out an investigating committee *to look into the disturbance* to find the cause of the unrest among the youth. Look into a mirror! The cause is you, Mr. and Mrs. Yesterday, you with your forked tongues.

A young white today cannot help but recoil from the base deeds of his people. On every side, on every continent, he sees racial arrogance, savage brutality toward the conquered and subjugated people, genocide; he sees the human cargo of the slave trade; he sees the systematic extermination of American Indians; he sees the civilized nations of Europe fighting in imperial depravity over the lands of other people — and over possession of the very people themselves. There seems to be no end to the ghastly deeds of which his people are guilty. *GUILTY*. The slaughter of the Jews by the Germans, the dropping of atomic bombs on the Japanese people — these deeds weigh heavily upon the prostrate souls and tumultuous consciences of the white youth. The white heroes, their hands dripping with blood, are dead.

The young whites know that the colored people of the world, Afro-Americans included, do not seek revenge for their suffering. They seek the same things the white rebel wants: an end to war and exploitation. Black and white, the young rebels are free people, free in a way that Americans have never been before in the history of their country. And they are outraged.

There is in America today a generation of white youth that is truly worthy of a black man's respect, and this is a rare event in the foul annals of American history. From the beginning of the contact between blacks and whites, there has been very little reason for a black man to respect a white, with such exceptions as John Brown and others lesser known. But respect commands itself and it can neither be given nor withheld when it is due. If a man like Malcolm X could change and repudiate racism, if I myself and other former Muslims can change, if young whites can change, then there is hope for America. It was certainly strange to find myself, while steeped in the doctrine that all whites were devils by nature, commanded by the heart to applaud and acknowledge respect for these young whites — despite the fact that they are descendants of the masters and I the descendant of slave. The sins of the fathers are visited upon the heads of the children — but only if the children continue in the evil deeds of the fathers.

FOR DISCUSSION

1. Cleaver says that young people today have new and different heroes from those of their parents. Who are your heroes? Are they different from those of your parents? If so, how do they differ?

2. Cleaver says: "The characteristics of the white rebels which most alarm their elders — the long hair, the new dances, their love for Negro music, their use of marijuana, their mystical attitude toward sex — are all tools of their rebellion." Explain what Cleaver means by tools. Do you think the tools he mentions are effective?

3. Cleaver describes Americans as "schizophrenic," as people who preach justice and practice intolerance. How does this sort of schizophrenia affect individuals as well as the whole nation?

4. Cleaver says that the "conflict between the generations. . . is deeper, even, than the struggle between the races." Do you agree? In the last paragraph Cleaver expresses hope that both conflicts can be favorably resolved. Does your experience cause you to be equally optimistic?